A CONVICTION IN QUESTION

The First Trial at the International Criminal Court

 **UTP** insights

UTP Insights is an innovative collection of brief books offering accessible introductions to the ideas that shape our world. Each volume in the series focuses on a contemporary issue, offering a fresh perspective anchored in scholarship. Spanning a broad range of disciplines in the social sciences and humanities, the books in the UTP Insights series contribute to public discourse and debate and provide a valuable resource for instructors and students.

BOOKS IN THE SERIES

A CONVICTION IN QUESTION

The First Trial at the International Criminal Court

Jim Freedman

UNIVERSITY OF TORONTO PRESS
Toronto Buffalo London

ISBN 978-1-4875-0289-8

Library and Archives Canada Cataloguing in Publication

Freedman, Jim, author
A conviction in question : the first trial at the International Criminal
Court / Jim Freedman.

(UTP insights)
Includes bibliographical references and index.
ISBN 978-1-4875-0289-8 (cloth)

1. Dyilo, Thomas Lubanga, 1960– – Trials, litigation, etc.   2. War criminals
– Congo (Democratic Republic).   3. War crimes – Congo (Democratic
Republic) – Ituri Region.   4. International Criminal Court.   5. Prosecution
(International law) – Case studies.   6. International criminal courts – Case
studies.   7. War crime trials – Netherlands – Hague – Case studies.   I. Title.
II. Series: UTP insights

KZ1216.D95F74 2017   341.6'90268   C2017-904752-3

University of Toronto Press acknowledges the financial assistance to its
publishing program of the Canada Council for the Arts and the Ontario Arts
Council, an agency of the Government of Ontario.

Canada Council   Conseil des Arts
for the Arts   du Canada

ONTARIO ARTS COUNCIL
CONSEIL DES ARTS DE L'ONT
an Ontario government agency
un organisme du gouvernement de l'(

Funded by the   Financé par le
Government   gouvernement
of Canada   du Canada

I am fully convinced that there is a common law among nations which is valid alike for war and in war. Throughout the Christian world I observed a lack of restraint in relation to war, such as even barbarous races should be ashamed of; I observed that men rush to arms for slight causes, or no cause at all, and that when arms have once been taken up there is no longer any respect for law, divine or human; it is as if, in accordance with a general decree, frenzy had openly been let loose for the committing of all crimes.

Hugo Grotius, *The Law of War and Peace*

Contents

Acknowledgments

Following the Thomas Lubanga affair from crime to conviction, from Eastern Congo to The Hague, to Belgium and France and Canada, and back to The Hague would have been quite impossible without the sympathetic collaboration of those who opened doors, advised, and informed along the way. Thanking them here is the least I can do. Luis Moreno-Ocampo, the original prosecutor, took an immediate interest in the book and recognized my presence at the International Criminal Court as a professional in residence. His interest was a gift. A journalist and trial monitor at the time, Sheila Vélez was assigned to help me with contacts, and she probably does not realize how helpful she was. I'll not list all of those in the Office of the Prosecution who spoke openly with me. Some, however, I must mention, such as Nicole Samson and Manoj Sachdeva, senior trial lawyers. At the very early stages of this project, Pascal Turlan, advisor to the Office of the Prosecution, was unusually insightful and understanding of my project. Paolina Massida, the principal counsel of the Office of the Public Counsel for Victims, made sure I had a firm grasp of the involvement of victims. Professor Valerie Oostervelt, associate dean in the Faculty of Law and a colleague at Western University in Canada, very kindly provided me with an initial introduction to the Court.

Nicolas Kuyaku, local spokesperson at the International Criminal Court facilities outside of Bunia, gave a warm welcome and a thoughtful account of the Court's presence in Ituri, northeast Congo.

The counsellor for the defence, Maître Catherine Mabille, agreed to meet with me in her Paris *cabinet*, even though she knew I strongly opposed her efforts to have him acquitted. She is a stalwart court warrior and commands considerable respect. The same goes for Counsellor Luc Walleyn, except Mr Walleyn has committed his practice and his life to defending human rights and was a uniquely principled presence in the trial. He was generous with his time and immensely helpful to me during our meeting in his Brussels office. My interview with Béatrice le Fraper du Hellen, who was deputy prosecutor and head of the Jurisdiction, Complementarity, and Co-operation Division at the time of the trial, was nothing short of remarkable. She is now France's ambassador to Malta. Finally and most particularly, there was my meeting with Professor William Schabas, a Canadian scholar of human rights law and arguably the most respected authority on the International Criminal Court and its proceedings. This is a woefully abridged list, but I trust all those who spoke with me and who assisted me in the course of this writing will accept my sincerest thanks.

My wife, Terilynn Graham, had a first read of the book, and I have to acknowledge she is one of the best editors I have ever encountered. I am lucky to have as a long-time friend Gary Moore, writer supreme, whose reading and comments are worth a king's ransom. And I am indebted finally to Daniel Quinlan at the University of Toronto Press, whose expert contributions were just what the book needed.

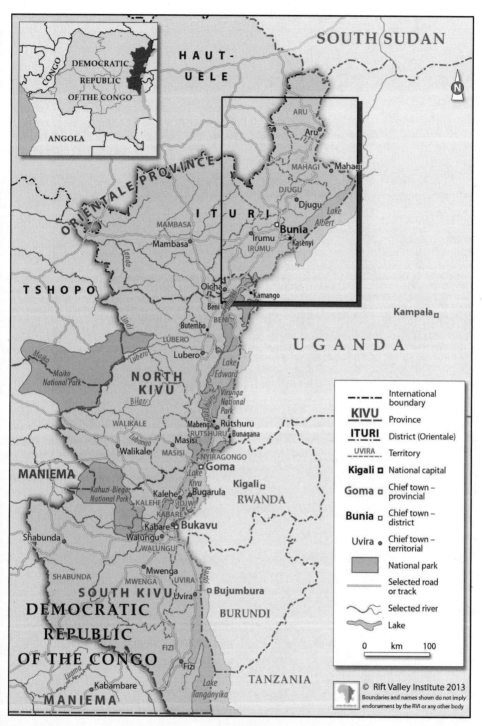

Map of Ituri in the Democratic Republic of the Congo
(permission of the Rift Valley Institute)

Introduction

The inaugural trial at the International Criminal Court of a notorious warlord from northeast Democratic Republic of the Congo was to be one for the history books. For decades, centuries even, regular citizens had had almost no legal refuge from the brutality of criminal rulers. There were the famous Nuremberg and Tokyo trials, but these were only two instances, and once the world saw what potent forces these courts could be and how they could reach deep into the customarily inviolate political centre of states and pull even heads of state into the dock, most states retreated. Until recently. There had been individual courts in Yugoslavia and Rwanda and elsewhere to prosecute criminals in individual nations, but these could only prosecute criminals from the countries for which the courts had been created. This Court and this trial were different. It was a Court for nearly all places and all times promising something most everyone in the world wanted badly, even if some state authorities remained wary. It was to bring tyrants to account, punish them according to their crimes, and give pause to others with tyrannical pretensions.

In its first trial, the International Criminal Court brought to The Hague a ruthless politician. Thomas Lubanga Dyilo (born 29 December 1960) had driven his ethnic militia to systematically exterminate neighbouring ethnic tribes in his part of the country known as Ituri. When these neighbouring groups pushed back, the result was an even more furious episode of bloodletting and sexual violence. His men carried atrocities to an extreme. For a short and very ugly time in 2002–3, Lubanga turned this corner of the Congo into a killing zone where, as one commentator put it, "All hell broke loose."[1]

Although he had committed a multitude of war crimes and crimes against humanity, he was charged only with using children under fifteen as soldiers, and for most of the trial this was the principal issue. Lubanga liked using children on the battlefield. They were loyal and easy to train, and as bodyguards they were fiercely protective, knowing their own lives depended on the preservation of his. He dressed the part of a warlord in flowing baby-blue robes that befitted a surrogate father commander. He liked the blind rush of the children into enemy lines, high on drugs, guns going off like cluster bombs. He especially liked how this mindless rush gave his manoeuvres a chaotic, out-of-control element. Lubanga was an educated person with a university degree and knew the internationals would object, but he suspected this kind of war could be waged largely free of international attention. He expected no one would notice if the men under his command forced their enemies to eat the body parts of their enemies, or if they seized women from anywhere and held them for months on end to serve their sexual pleasure, or if they systematically mutilated citizens to let everyone know he was the ruler of the region, or if he conscripted young children to fight for him and drugged them so they would have no idea what they were doing.

But this time, the world did take notice. Lubanga rose to power on the tail end of six years of war following the overthrow of the president-for-life Mobutu Sese Seko (1930–97), a tumultuous period that exposed the country to international attention as legions of humanitarians and peacekeepers came in to provide assistance and keep the peace. They were watching as Lubanga rose to power. It was in that same year, 2002, that the treaty laying the foundation for the new International Criminal Court received the requisite number of ratifications to bring the Court fully into being. There was now a world court with jurisdiction over genocide, crimes against humanity, war crimes, and crimes of aggression no matter where they occurred. Not long after, the Court began to cast about for a perpetrator notorious enough to make for an uncomplicated first trial, and Thomas Lubanga was the one. By early 2004, Lubanga had been captured and incarcerated by the Congolese government, and when the Office of the Prosecution broached the matter of bringing him to The Hague for the Court's first trial, the government agreed. He was arrested and transferred to The Hague in March 2006.

This book is a story of the trial that begins with the crimes themselves and ends with the verdict. It is for the most part a non-fiction narrative with the occasional academic digression, though because I witnessed much of what is written and became embroiled in the events themselves, it is also, in part, a memoir. It happened that a "Panel of Experts" had been assembled under the auspices of the United Nations to keep track of why and where fighting persisted in the DR Congo where Lubanga was prominently on the radar, and I served on this panel. It was in the course of my visits to Ituri, beginning in June 2002 while Lubanga's men were readying themselves, that I saw first-hand what he was doing. He had struck a deal with the Ugandan armed forces to have their support, and day-by-day, I sensed the spread of dread throughout the region. He was going to assassinate the local governor, President Kabila's man in the region. He was going to raze any settlement that was not Hema. He was going to kill anyone who had supported Kabila's government, and somewhere in his plans he intended to set himself up as ruler over an autonomous Ituri region. These were the soaring delusions of a man possessed of his own personal grandeur.

It was alarming to witness these events. It was not as if it was anything new in a world where episodes of violent conflict have become increasingly common and in truth, over decades of advising international organizations, I have witnessed a few. It was that this outbreak of internecine conflict precipitated by Lubanga was especially lethal. My interest gravitated towards these events for they were indeed exceptional, and then once the Court was ready to begin proceedings, I followed the trial. It would have been hard not to. I was curious about what the new Court would make of the case, whether it could in fact reckon with these crimes, some of which I had by chance observed. I wondered whether the lofty vision of the Court inscribed in the Rome Statute could deal with the harsh reality of what Lubanga had done in Ituri. It was not just what kind of justice would be rendered for Lubanga. The Court itself was on trial.

This was no small matter. It had taken almost fifty years after the landmark war crimes trials at Nuremberg and Tokyo before sovereign states would allow a world court to reach into their internal affairs and prosecute their citizens. Planning for a world court laboured for decades, largely in obscurity. But as wars around the world increased in the 1990s, so did the need for some kind of a global court to hold those responsible to account. When a conference of states finally approved the idea at the Rome Conference in 1998, followed by the requisite number of state ratifications, and when in 2006 the first defendant from the Ituri region of the Democratic Republic of Congo was arrested and brought to trial in The Hague, a momentous new era was ushered in. Nothing like it had ever occurred. The previously closed curtains of state sovereignty were drawn open and there, on the world stage, was the first ever international judiciary.

I followed the trial and whenever possible spent extended periods in The Hague sitting and watching from the public gallery. I was there for the key moments when the gallery was full, and I was there during the long, seemingly interminable doldrums of cross-examinations by the defence team when I was the only public observer. I laboured with the transcripts, which was an especially challenging endeavour since they were not organized in any obvious fashion at the time, and many of them were redacted, presumably for security reasons. The prosecutor, Luis Moreno-Ocampo, granted me the status of professional-in-residence and encouraged those involved with the Lubanga case to speak openly. Maître Mabille, chief counsel for the defence, agreed to spend a morning with me in her cabinet in Paris, as did Luc Walleyn, counsellor for the victims, in his Brussels office. There were others: NGO advocates, counsellors in the Office of the Prosecution, staff from the Victim and Witnesses Unit, and more.

I have written this account in the first person. I am not a legal scholar, either by profession or by inclination. This is instead an unapologetically eyewitness account of the Lubanga trial from crime to conviction. I do not pretend there is any other authority for this account apart from my own conscientiousness as a narrator, and I say this knowing there will be some who will, on this account at least, dismiss it out of hand. I am nevertheless convinced this way of telling the story is the most appropriate, for rendering what transpired since observing the events and the trial by following the trace of prominent legal issues does not tell very much. It certainly does not tell why the trial was so troubling to so many observers from a diversity of angles – political or legal.

This is not a study in any event. It is a story. It is the story of a trial that, at the beginning, seemed to me and probably to others to have had a reasonably expectable outcome. Lubanga's atrocities spoke for themselves, or so it appeared. They were well known in his home country. They were well known abroad among the international organizations that had been forced to intervene to protect his victims, and they were well known among human rights organizations whose reporting brought his crimes to world attention. Something would have to go woefully askew for the trial to end up questioning the severity of the crimes. And yet, as the trial unfolded, the crimes became strangely and increasingly beside the point, buried under a spectacle of legal combat between counsellors who seemed more concerned with prevailing in the courtroom than worrying about what atrocities had been committed in Ituri and how to assign responsibility.

It is a strange story as trials go. The length of time it took to arrive at a conclusion, six years in total, is nothing short of peculiar. The judge's determination to stop the proceedings and send Lubanga home, not once but twice, was also strange, not to mention the laborious appeals that reversed the judge's decisions. The discord in the Chamber is worthy of a lurid television series. The main actors in the Chamber turned even the most innocent of evidence into something hotly contested, generating a cacophony of opposing voices that drowned out much of what the Court needed to know to make an informed decision. The Chamber often saw fit to allow factual and moral matters to be trumped by other matters.

Not too many people around the Court wanted to talk about how unseemly the behaviour of the key actors had become. It was a taboo topic as far as I could see, though there were quite a few who seemed to feel as I did. The prosecutor himself, I think, was one of those concerned by the direction the trial was headed in, and he was willing to speak openly; it certainly did not unfold as he expected and, if I asked, he spoke honestly about his discomfort with the proceedings. There were others in the Office of the Prosecution who were dismayed, and only sometime after the trial's conclusion have they been willing to speak about it. Those who had a lesser stake in the outcome often raised their hands in exasperation and let me see their frustration. But there was one individual whom I hold in the greatest respect, though I knew him only briefly, who was particularly eloquent on the matter. He happened to have been the scribe of the trial, a writer of some repute hired by the prosecutor to write the trial's account. He was in residence at the Court for two years before, out of frustration and distaste for what was going on, he resigned and wrote his own book. His name is Gil Courtemanche and his book was *Le Monde, le lézard et moi*.

It is a thinly disguised fictional account of the trial and its outcome. In the book, Lubanga is acquitted, as the author suspected he might be and as others whom he knew and worked with also suspected, and he, the narrator, is horrified. After the acquittal and after Lubanga returns to Ituri, the narrator experiences a deep depression at the abridgment of justice, and he travels to Ituri to observe Lubanga as a free man. It is the story of a man deeply injured by the injustice of it all and, in the wake of everything, descends into a personal crisis precipitated by the Court's failure to deal with human evil.

Courtemanche's book was published in 2010, well before the trial was concluded. Gil Courtemanche was already ill at the time, and he passed away in 2011. I dedicate this book to his memory.

Jim Freedman
2016

A Note on Dialogue

Where dialogue appears in quotes, it is a verbatim rendering of a conversation or a close approximation. I made every effort to record discussions word for word while taking notes or, if this was impossible, to write down what transpired immediately afterwards. Though there may be an inadvertent error or two, these dialogues are very close to the actual conversations. Verbatim dialogue appears occasionally throughout the book, including interactions with the United Nations peacekeepers in Ituri, conversations with the governor of Ituri, Jean-Pierre Molondo Lompondo, interviews with the legal representative for the victims, Luc Walleyn, with Béatrice de Fraper du Hellen in the Office of the Prosecution, and others. Where the dialogues do not appear in quotes, the conversations are approximations but are not verbatim. On the occasion where these dialogues originally took place in French, the translations are my own.

Trial dialogue is taken directly from the transcripts, which are available on the International Criminal Court's website. Where the original discussion or interrogation took place in French, I have used the English translation available in the English transcripts.

A CONVICTION IN QUESTION

The First Trial at the International Criminal Court

chapter 1

The Way to Bunia

TMK Commuter airline operating in the northeast corner of the DR Congo was hardly my preference for travelling from Goma to Bunia, the capital of Ituri, in mid-July 2002. The plane frequently overshot the small runways it served in northeast DR Congo and, on one occasion in September 1997, its one and only aircraft crashed into a hillside, killing all nineteen persons on board. But the alternatives were not good. Travelling by road northeast from Goma to Bunia was nearly impossible. The road was little more than a dirt track, and even if an all-terrain vehicle could get through, which was doubtful, there would be armed men every fifty kilometres taking a twenty-dollar service fee before you could pass. If that is all they wanted, you were lucky. Travelling with the United Nations airplane network took three days flying cross-country to Kinshasa, and the next day to Kisangani, and then a helicopter to Bunia. And it was not the money really, or the time, but the papers one was expected to fill out and the stamps required from bleary-eyed internationals suffering from Congo's unrelenting torpor. With TMK I could make Bunia in a morning. On most days the plane took off around eight and landed first in Butembo, then in Beni, then Bunia, and, after Bunia, made a brief stop in Entebbe airport in Uganda before retracing its steps to Goma in the evening.

The ticket office had moved since the last time I'd flown, and no one at the Goma International Airport seemed to know where it was, so on the afternoon before what I hoped would be my departure, I greeted the returning TMK plane and collared a passenger. Directions were sketchy – back corner of a warehouse somewhere past the turnoff to the Karibu Hotel and don't take the turnoff, just keep going straight after the circle, past a beauty shop. It wasn't right there, but someone at the beauty shop knew someone who knew, and it was, as I'd learned, located in the far corner of an abandoned storage building where a flirty young girl was painting her nails while a cluster of would- be clients were yelling at her in a mixture of Swahili and French. I joined the crowd, and, after some belligerence and flirting, the young girl passed over to the crowd a crumpled handful of tickets to fill out. She said she would stamp them once payment was made.

There was only one pilot as far as I could tell, and he choreographed his flights in precisely the same way day after day. He placed his foot on the step into the plane in precisely the same movement. Papers were strewn on the dashboard the same way every day, and he tapped the gauges in precisely the same fashion as if none of them worked without a wake-up call. He flew the same trajectory, leaning into the Nyiragongo crater heading north the same way every time, his ponderous flight following the roads below into Butembo that might have been navigable before the decade of war. In Butembo the runway was too short, and each time he touched down inches from where the grassy field started, he reversed the pitch of the propellers, gunning the engine with precisely the same roar until the plane settled with a thud inches from the end of a slippery uphill slope. There we were greeted by the mayor, who apologized with the same mellifluous grace every time, promising an improved strip soon. Leaving Butembo, we headed for Beni, where the pilot navigated a similarly tricky strip that made him come in low with a terrifying roar of the engine, leaning into the strip and finally pulling the plane up to catch the upward slope. The final thirty seconds to touchdown were bone chilling as our pilot seemed to point the aircraft directly at the ground, roaring headlong into the earth as passengers craned their necks in unison to see through the cockpit window where the banana groves' remote blotches of green with their blur of fronds were rushing in to us, until, at the last minute, the plane pulled up onto the red, dun incline, slamming into the uphill strip at just the right speed to carry us along the runway. A little trailer served as an airport. It was nothing much really, but there was always a crowd, a collection of Greek merchants, Belgian businessmen, women of the night, counterfeiters, and would-be politicians. In Beni, this was the place and time to be seen.

The airstrip belonged to the Belgian Robert Ducarme, who had settled in Beni years before, where he had set up an operation to extract papain, a digestive enzyme, from his papaya groves. He had done reasonably well, processing the harvest in a small local factory and shipping it off for sale in Europe through Nairobi. Over the years, he became the impresario of Beni, if there could be such a thing. He had built a park adjacent to his factory, where there were gracious houses, his own most prominently, and others held by politicians and Greek fishermen and the odd diamond merchant. It was an idyll in the midst of a turbulent landscape.

At Beni we were two-thirds of the way to Bunia. There was often such a gathering at the Beni airport, as if we were all dignitaries and so much so that even for those of us going on it seemed we had come to the end of our journey. Robert Ducarme was nearly always on hand to greet the morning plane, for he was indeed the airport's owner, a one-man traveller's aid booth and information kiosk, baggage official, and chair of the Chamber of Commerce to welcome business visitors and ensure their needs were met in genteel fashion. He knew nearly everyone travelling, the long-time residents, the Greeks still there after generations, bankers and traders and those reborn under the sign of Jesus, the political pretenders and the born-in-Beni owners of the new motel who gave lodging to friends and their prostitutes, men in their cups and ladies in their lingerie. There would be nothing like this at the next stop in Bunia, nothing to compare with Mr Ducarme himself, or the coterie of self-proclaimed politicians in their large black cars with their paramours and the schoolmarms with their children who came to the airport in the morning to watch the spectacular landing and the passengers deplane. The passengers milled around shaking hands and swapping stories. There was occasionally a tray of snacks laid on, and finally the hour would come to depart when the chocks under the wheels would be thrown to the side and M Ducarme's cargo for the day loaded in the back, while one by one the passengers tucked away their fine dispositions and, with regret, again mounted the TMK plane for the next leg into the volatile land of Ituri, where the capital Bunia was very much another story. The new arrivals and their welcomers would stay to watch the airplane plummet just as wildly down the strip, leaving the ground in a dramatic flourish out of Beni at breakneck speed, barely enough at the end of the runway to float above the treetops. Meanwhile, inside the plane, passengers looked around to see just who'd gotten back on board. They would all have to have a good reason.

Bunia is more populated than Beni, larger and more moneyed, and it is not just digestive enzymes that bring in the income. In Ituri it is gold. There are diamonds in the interior, rare minerals, and animals. It was the last stop before Uganda where gold and diamonds were easily laundered by the South Asian traders who had friends in Dubai and Abu Dhabi and Antwerp. There was frequent fighting over these riches, which had turned Bunia into a mean sort of town, a cauldron of ethnic animosities that had been brewing, some say, for half a decade, others say for half a century, the perfect cover for a pillaging and smuggling operation.

Bunia's approach was plain by comparison with the others, save for the arresting sight to the left of the plane where a field of Ugandan soldiers were literally dug in, lodged in shallow earthen trenches under makeshift shelters. From my window, I had a bird's-eye view. A few of the hundreds of encampments on the field had tents or makeshift cloth sheets to cover their lodgings, others had pilfered pieces of wood and any scrap at hand to cover the holes they had dug into the earth, perhaps for privacy, as if, by sinking themselves into a hole, they staked a more serious claim. It was a motley camp: some were hanging clothes, others were brandishing their weapons, others carrying water or simply sitting, transistor radio in hand. One might have thought the Uganda People's Defence Force, the national army, would have found a more discreet encampment, since these Ugandan squaddies, in truth, had come to this part of the Congo uninvited to play a pirate's game, to prey on the place. The better armed would sell protection to truckers and diamond merchants. Others seized whatever they could.

Not many of us were deplaning that day: an Indian man come to buy gold; a man who claimed to be a banker from Kinshasa in a three-piece suit; a woman under wild dreadlocks, laden with cheap electronics. There was no one to position the chocks under the wheels. There was no one to greet the new arrivals, few as we were; no vehicles to be seen, not even a wagon for carrying the bags that the pilot tossed on the ground as if to say good riddance, leaving me to shoulder my backpack and drag a small duffel to the pock-marked, baby-blue concrete hut of an airport. The place was deserted.

No sooner were the bags on the ground than the pilot turned the plane around and, in a farewell roar, departed northeast towards Entebbe, careening over the lakes and green hills and leaving an eerie quiet to settle over the airport.

The banker in the three-piece suit walked to the road leading to town, flagged down a motorcycle, and sped away. The lady with the dreadlocks sauntered off towards the Ugandan army camp, humming and jiggling the string of electronics draped over her neck and shoulders. A small pickup appeared in a few minutes to scoop up the Indian man, and shortly afterward, a bevy of curious young Ugandan soldiers in the back of a pickup with lips slathered in seeds from drinking sorghum homebrew caromed around in a dusty haze, waving their guns in the air. After they left and all of the other passengers had departed, the conditions of this airstrip came fully into view. There were quasi-craters in the macadam and rusting shrapnel from debris no one had bothered to collect, signs of fighting not so long ago. The derelict little airport structure was scarred and covered with bullet holes.

The shrapnel and the debris were the remnants of the conflict I was there to observe. There had been fighting throughout the DR Congo since 1998, war in the South and the West and the East, and here in the Northeast especially. And while there were different aggressors in every part of the country, the theme running through the conflicts everywhere was the search for loot, gold and timber and diamonds, the precious metal tantalum, and even ivory. Ituri was famous for its gold deposits; there were diamonds in the surrounding areas and valuable hardwood timber in the hinterlands, and as long as the central government in Kinshasa was paralysed by nationwide chaos, rogue elements from the Ugandan army in Ituri were seizing and selling what they could get their hands on. But in Ituri there was something more. To get access to the minerals and the trees, rogue units of the Ugandan forces had allied with one local ethnic group or another, with the result that tension between ethnic groups that had once been latent now erupted into full-scale fighting. It was the game plan of the Ugandans; they liked the cover this combat gave their criminal operations. Ethnic group leaders who might have tried to stop the Ugandans did the opposite and played into their hands by using them for their own political ends. The most notorious was the leader of the Hema ethnic group, Thomas Lubanga. Lubanga preached and plotted the extermination of a neighbouring ethnic group, the Lendu, and allied with the Ugandan soldiers-turned-mercenaries to arm his fighters to attack Lendu villages. The Lendu understandably fought back, and day by day the situation was getting worse.

Conflict had reached new levels shortly before my arrival. In retaliation for Hema attacks in Lendu areas, Lendu armed men had attacked a Hema town southeast of Bunia where the community had built a 400-bed hospital with help from abroad. The Lendu were furious and their attack was relentless. They killed patients and doctors alike. The Hema's Ugandan allies brought in a Russian-made Mi-17 helicopter gunship to strafe the attackers; the Lendu withdrew and the helicopter returned to the Bunia airport. A few days later the Lendu fighters regrouped and stormed the airport with guns and grenades aimed at destroying the helicopter gunship parked there. They partially succeeded, leaving the pieces of metal I saw scattered around the tarmac.

Beyond the wreckage and past the derelict airport structure I could hear the din rising from the encampment of Ugandans, a modulated hum of voices with an occasional outburst. Girls were walking in and out of the area. I could see the men's uniforms in the distance, brown khakis and camouflage and, of course, the coveted boots. The woman with the electronics was somewhere in this sprawling maze of raucous soldiers, hawking her wares, showing her headphones and bags of pirated CDs and miniature players. Even from a distance I could see there was none of the discipline that armies usually have. This was not really an army, even though they were soldiers in Uganda's national armed forces with the emblem of the Ugandan People Defence Force blazoned below the epaulets next to company emblems. In the camp they were divided into small groups working for one officer or another, each with their own mercenary operations. One group might be deployed to subdue a community or eliminate some discontents while another might be sent to escort a shipment of tusks plundered from the game park.

They camped together to give the illusion they were there on an official peacekeeping mission. In truth they were there on business. The dreadlocks lady knew this, and she would soon emerge from the camp to wait on the tarmac for the TMK Commuter to return from Entebbe and take her back to Goma with a bag full of cash. These men were there to make money, and their commanders, most of them friends and relatives of the Ugandan President Museveni, were there to make large amounts of money. They cared little if, in the process, they stoked the violence and ethnic hatreds in Ituri, for it was by keeping the conflict alive and the insecurity high that the Ugandans ensured that both the Hema and the Lendu relied on the Ugandans for guns and protection. This, in turn, gave the Ugandans an excuse to stay in the area, and they could carry on their businesses without arousing suspicion.

At first the United Nations looked away while the Ugandan military took the economy hostage, pillaging under the guise of peacekeeping. The government of the DRC had only the sketchiest presence in Ituri, hardly enough to calm the escalating tensions or keep the Ugandan soldiers from taking the gold or the diamonds or cattle or from pillaging households for chicken and grain. International NGOs objected to what the Ugandans were doing and wrote reports chronicling the stranglehold the Ugandans had over the economy and how they pitted one ethnic group against another. Church groups and international organizations raised a cry, pleading with the United Nations Security Council to do something. There was no one to stop them. The Security Council could not agree on what to do, and when the president of Uganda, Yoweri Museveni, promised he would instruct his soldiers to keep the peace in the region, Security Council members said fine and looked the other way.

Members of the Security Council knew well enough what was going on. They had seen the pattern before in other problem spots where renegade forces financed their pillaging and incidentally fuelled the conflict by selling off resources, trees, minerals, precious stones, and parts of endangered animal species. Opposing forces in Angola had financed their fighting with the sale of diamonds from local kimberlite deposits. Liberian soldiers under Charles Taylor financed their collaboration with rebels to control Sierra Leone's diamond fields by marketing trees and precious stones. Members of the Security Council agreed on very little, but they could agree at least on sending a team of investigators to the DR Congo, as they had done in Angola and Sierra Leone. They called this team a Panel of Experts, a new instrument for the Security Council. Angola had a Panel of Experts reporting on how the diamond trade fuelled the fighting. There was another one reporting on the events in Liberia and Sierra Leone, and now there was this one for the Democratic Republic of the Congo. My job was to draw a line connecting the rebels and their guns to the theft of resources in the northern stretch of Congo's border to the East.

How now, I wondered, perched on the veranda of this abandoned airport building, would I piece all this together? Just then a white Toyota Land Cruiser bearing blue UN letters spun onto the tarmac and squealed to a stop in front of the place where I was waiting. There was barely time to think. Two armed men in blue peacekeeper helmets jumped from the vehicle as if storming a beach and seized my bags, pushing me uncomfortably towards a rear door.

With his burly hand around my arm, the Senegalese commander stopped short. A high-ranking Ugandan officer stepped from the makeshift baggage area behind us to see the commotion. He had a pistol. The Senegalese jerked his head in the man's direction as a sign for me to have a look.

I was placed firmly inside. We drove out in a swirl of dust along the road to town lined with women carrying water on their heads, with children in tow. The driver, a Kenyan, spoke first.

"Good day sir."

"Good day."

"Sorry for the delay. Clearance. We had an exchange of gunfire here yesterday. Nineteen hundred hours."

"Where?"

"Here, sir, at the airport."

"Lubanga's men?"

"No sir, the governor's.

"Molondo Lompondo?"

"Correct. Our intelligence has informed that Lubanga's group paid the Ugandan commander we just saw 150 thousand dollars for him to get rid of the governor. That was the man you just saw, General Peter Karim. To remove the governor, sir."

"Remove?"

"Assassinate."

"And the governor?" I presumed he was still alive, since I was to meet him in an hour.

"The governor is in a difficult situation. He is an honest man, the government's man, if you will, but the situation is … well, you see, the Ugandans have their own motives here and, for the moment, they are not to support the governor. Or at least not at the present time. You must have heard of the Hema sir, the group seeking power. It is a tense situation and with this Thomas Lubanga leading the Hema, the situation has deteriorated. We would not advise a meeting with the governor at this time."

"Thank you."

"You are most welcome to Bunia. In better times we would be pleased to have visitors, to facilitate in a better fashion."

"I am nevertheless scheduled to visit the governor shortly."

"You are under our protection, sir."

"Then wait at the governor's office."

"That would be risky," said the Senegalese commander riding shotgun, reaching for his weapon.

"Then I'll return on my own."

We turned onto the main road for the two kilometres into town and flew around a corner to the right, as if to throw someone off our tail, even though there was no one in the streets, took another right to the side of the road next to base compound for the eight resident peacekeepers.

Gunfire could be heard in the streets. There was only a handful of peacekeepers, far too few to make any difference to anyone.

"People think we can protect them and we cannot," said the commander. "Only puts us in harm's way. It's the Ugandans in charge. No need to tell you what you already saw at the airport, and there is very little the eight of us can do. The Hema are a dangerous group and you should understand this. Lubanga stops at nothing. They want to control Ituri, get rid of the Lendu, and one day secede from the Congo. And the Ugandan army is backing them, though, if you ask me, they are just playing with them. The Hema think they are the only ones to rule Ituri. They think the governor, the man you are about to see, is Kabila's man. And what's worse, they think he is protecting the Lendu. And, remember, the Hema aim is to eliminate the Lendu. They will kill the governor. No one knows when it will happen. It could be today, and now you tell us you want to talk to him this afternoon. Fine, my friend, talk with the governor. We hope you know what you are doing, because the governor – decent fellow, I'll give you that – he's in a tough spot. His place is ground zero."

⌒

This was my second visit to Ituri. Members of the Panel of Experts were discouraged from travelling on their own, and perhaps I should not have come this time, or at least not alone. But the reports were ominous about the conflict in Ituri becoming dramatically worse, and if we were to wait any longer, there might be a full-scale war and a full-scale evacuation that would make a visit impossible. We would know little of what was needed to bring this emerging calamity to the Security Council's attention. The governor, Jean-Pierre Molondo Lompondo, and I had struck up a friendship in the course of my first visit. He was a man of honour and some education. He had seen many conflicts in his long career, and Lubanga's reckless drive for power was nothing new to him. The governor was committed to exposing what was happening in this corner of the world and he hoped the Security Council would take notice. That was, as he told me during my last visit, where our group came in.

He confessed he might be wrong. He was that kind of a man, contemplative and, unlike other officers in his position, not overly self-assured. Museveni might eventually realize how grotesque the schemes of his men were and what an alliance with Lubanga might do to his reputation. He might recall his men, and that would end the xenophobic march of the Hema, who would then have only the bare bones of their own small militia, not enough to carry out their outrageous plan to exterminate their neighbours. But if the Ugandans stayed allied with Lubanga as he unleashed his plans, that was another thing. It would be a bloodbath. There was no reason to count on the so-called peacekeepers holed up in their compound.

He needed someone from the UN to pay attention. No one of our group doubted it. In June, reports of violence in Ituri began to come into our offices in Nairobi from NGOs and UN staff stationed there. And then the phone call from the Governor's Office, nearly inaudible, requesting a second visit. The head of our Panel was against it at first. He was against a member travelling alone, but he could not deny the obligation to render an account, especially if we were the only ones.

chapter 2

Museveni's Divide and Plunder

The violent clashes between Thomas Lubanga's group of Hema and other ethnicities in the region that erupted in Ituri spun out of a series of violent events and military adventures that had engulfed much of Central Africa. It began when Rwanda and Uganda combined forces in 1996 to march on Kinshasa and overthrow Congo's long-ruling despot, Mobutu Sese Seko. With Mobutu gone, they put Laurent (Le Père) Kabila in power, on the assumption that Kabila would be Kagame's "man in the Congo." But as soon as Kabila was in power, it was clear he would be no one's puppet – neither Kagame's nor Museveni's. Kagame was not pleased. In 1998, Rwanda and Uganda once again joined forces to teach Kabila a lesson, but this time it backfired. Kabila fought back, and Angola and Zimbabwe came in to support him. Now there were six African countries at war on Congolese soil: Rwanda, Uganda, and Burundi on one side, and Congo, Zimbabwe, and Angola on the other; it bordered on chaos. Zimbabwe and Angola might have been there on the pretence of supporting Kabila, but it was only a pretence. In reality, their troops used this as an excuse to stay in the Congo and steal its riches. It was the same for Rwanda and Uganda; they cared less about Congolese politics than they did about looting the mines in the East. The war, if it can be called a war, went on for six years, with forces allied to Kabila and those against swarming like carrion birds over the weak animal of the Congo.[1] It was officially over in 2002, but it was years before some of the armed groups returned to their home countries.

Kagame never had any intention of pulling his men out of the DR Congo. They set themselves up as rebel rulers in a large portion of the East. Uganda's plans were different, initially at least, as they made their way wearily home through Mbandaka in Equateur and Kisangani in Orientale Province towards Ituri, a few days' march from their border. But there, in Ituri, something changed. Here was a region fully on the other side of the country from Kinshasa and dripping with riches. They saw diamonds exchanging hands, gold sold by small traders, and no police in Bunia or any government to speak of. Armed as they were, it was easy to take what they wanted. There was rare timber and elephant tusks and animals from the game parks and crops and cattle from hapless farmers. There was an economy that needed fuel whose import they could control and, in time, the Ugandan soldiers, under a cadre of officers-turned-warlords, came to bring most exports and imports under their direct control. They stayed, and if anyone asked, they said they were there to keep the peace in an unruly area. In truth, it was as if a criminal gang had seized an entire economy with guns and mortars and took to pillaging at will.

Museveni allowed his favourite soldiers to remain in Ituri, where they seized valuable commodities and sold them for handsome profits, a portion for themselves and a portion for him. A few officers dealt in gemstones, others in precious metals, and others in wood, while some simply seized goods off the shelves of local shop owners. Different assets in different locales led the Ugandans to strike deals with the ethnic groups on site for labour and collusion, and for this the Ugandan soldiers made deals, some with the Hema tribal group, some with the Lendu, and some with the Ngiti. If they needed transport in a place where a Hema family had land and trucks, they would make a deal, and if, in return, the Hema landowner wanted the Ugandan soldiers to run some Lendu off neighbouring land, the Ugandans did it. In turn, if Lendu or Ngiti collaborators needed protection, there were Ugandan soldiers available for hire. For the Ugandans, these were business opportunities, and if there were political consequences, so be it. For the Hema and the Lendu and the Ngiti and others in Ituri, it turned into a deadly game.

There had been some tension for years between the Hema and the Lendu, though nothing that would justify a full-scale war. It had started with the politics of the Belgian colonists who chose the Hema as their favourites and gave them access to favoured local jobs while others were treated as inferior. Resentment was unavoidable.[2] Few of the Hema or the Lendu took it seriously. They had been neighbours for centuries, they had intermarried, and there was little to tell them apart, if indeed there ever was. And yet some of the Hema convinced themselves over the years that they were descended from the superior stock of Nilotic herdsmen in Central Africa who migrated from northern Africa and dominated the Bantu wherever they settled. There is no evidence for this mythical genealogy, but some of the prouder Hema came to think of themselves as Nilotes and lords of the land, and even now, Hema professors at the university in Bunia fervently teach Hema's superior origins as bona fide history, as if it were foreordained that Hema should rule in Ituri by right of race and blood.

The Ugandan mercenaries took advantage of this simmering resentment for their own purposes, to play one group off against another. Tensions between the Hema and the Lendu mounted encounter by encounter. There was the case of Singa Kodjo, a wealthy, self-righteous Hema landowner who, in April 1999, seized the lands of a neighbouring Lendu community and taunted them. At the same time, Kodjo engaged the mercenary commander of the local Ugandan forces to stand at the ready when the Lendu took the bait. The Ugandan mercenaries did what they had agreed to do: they killed the Lendus, forced them from their homes and their land.

The Ugandans made little attempt to conceal what they were doing in Ituri, as if strangling an economy with its myriad consequences was of minor importance. It was only day by day that I came to see it for what it was during my first visit in April 2002. It seemed so improbable at first that a foreign occupier would capture the market of so many of a region's principal commodities while pretending to operate a functioning government, collecting licences and fees and charging levies with no intention of delivering any services. All this while abetting a civil war. The Ugandan commanders were even somewhat lackadaisical about it. Some even assisted with our investigation into their illegal exploitations, confiding that so-and-so commander used the Lendu to fell tropical hardwood in the forests they sent for milling in Uganda, as if it was as incongruous to them as it was to us. Or they had heard that some Ugandan soldiers had participated in a raid south of Bunia on the town of Gety. Too small a matter to merit any long political justification, though scores of people had died.

Even President Museveni appeared to lack much of a political agenda for his men in the northeast Congo, at least not one so coherent as Kagame's in Rwanda. Kagame had put Laurent Kabila in power in Kinshasa after Mobutu was gone and expected Kabila to return the favour by letting Kagame have his way in the vast and chaotic east. Kagame wanted to establish a foothold in North and South Kivu; he would finance his imperialist operations by taking Congo's minerals and gemstones to market as if they were his own. Since the eastern provinces were so geographically removed from faraway Kinshasa, he hoped one day to find a way to make parts of the Eastern Congo his own, maybe even a Rwandan protectorate. It was different with Museveni and the Ugandans. The officers could do as they wished. There was no grand design. But the consequences of Uganda's haphazard exploitation of Ituri were as grave as Rwanda's unabashed imperialism.

The Ugandans made alliances here and there with Hema and Lendu and others as long as the alliances and the ploys served their purpose for extricating what assets could be removed. Museveni personally liked the Hema because the name for his own tribe, the Hima, sounded similar, and he fancied the two of them were somehow kin and shared what was thought to be superior Nilotic stock. He decided initially he would put Hema in charge. He had to do something to show he was trying to keep the peace as a cover for his men's commercial exploits, and he knew the international community would be watching and would disapprove if they discovered Uganda's presence in Ituri was actually abetting ethnic conflict. Museveni threw his support first behind a woman, a notoriously proud Hema. Not surprisingly, she had little popular support and was soon forced out of office. He changed tactics after that. He made himself out to be a mediator, and for this he summoned to Kampala three Ituri figures who had pretentions to power. One was a Hema who had run the state gold-mining operation and had political aspirations. Another was Mbusa Nyamwisi from an important local family who was conspicuously not a Hema and was perceived to favour non-Hema tribes, including the Lendu. A third was Professor Wamba dia Wamba, who might have managed to reconcile the two others had he possessed more local standing, but it was a futile endeavour. None of the three could have handled Ituri on his own, much less collectively, and the alliance was a lost cause from the beginning. Museveni would have to try something else.

He liked the young Thomas Lubanga, as long as Lubanga did not get too serious about exterminating his enemies or purifying Ituri of the "lesser tribes." Word might get out and attract too much negative attention. Museveni did not want to hear anything about Hemas and Lendus, and he did not want an all-out war under his watch – it was all too sensitive – and anyway, as far as he was concerned, his occupation of Ituri was all about the loot.[3] The efforts he made to cobble together a semblance of political order were never more than half-hearted.

Meanwhile, antagonisms in Ituri grew. The support Museveni offered the Hema gave them the illusion that they could run roughshod over others and could rule all of Ituri as they had always imagined they should. Lubanga fancied himself a prince among the Hemas and future ruler of the region. The Hema leaders founded a political party, the Union des Patriotes Congolais, and Lubanga's reputation grew. At the same time his arch-opponent, Mbusa Nyamisi, gained the support of Kabila in Kinshasa, and he too wielded power in Ituri. This alliance between Mbusa and Kabila did not amount to much, but it was enough to distance Mbusa further from Lubanga and to push Lubanga's resolve even more to make Ituri an independent Hema state under his command. Between 2001 and 2002, Mbusa and Lubanga moved closer and closer to a state of war, and Museveni turned a blind eye, hoping the situation would fizzle out on its own.

But Thomas Lubanga Dyilo would not go away. In the early years of Ugandan occupation between 1998 and 2000 Lubanga had been a local strongman hungry for power. That was when Museveni calculated he could do business with him. Lubanga was invited to Uganda in 2000 with his gang of Hema toughs, boy soldiers, and followers in tow for training at the premier Ugandan training camps in Kyankwanzi and Jinja, and the commanders were impressed with what they saw: an educated young man who was politically astute. They could use a leader like him to calm the escalating tensions in Ituri which were gaining international attention. But that was before they saw him in action. What they saw was a reckless penchant for doling out violence with such abandon his group became known as Al Qaeeda of Ituri. Museveni came to worry his men might have to reckon with these Hema extremists once they began to upset the delicate balance among ethnic groups the Ugandans wanted to maintain. In addition, there were too many Tutsi in Lubanga's group for Museveni's taste, for he suspected this meant they were taking orders from Kagame's dreaded pro-Rwanda government in Kigali. Museveni preferred to ignore Lubanga as long as he could – until, that is, he became impossible to ignore.

The turning point came when Mbusa Nyamwisi, Lubanga's archrival and a man of influence in Ituri, urged President Kabila in Kinshasa to install a senior soldier as his man and governor in Ituri. He was Jean-Pierre Molondo Lompondo. This was the man I was to see in an hour. It was Mbusa's way of deliberately pushing Lubanga to the margins of the political picture, and Lubanga was furious. Lubanga and his men readied themselves for all-out war. He made his position clear in a statement in April 2002 when he said Mbusa was plotting a takeover of Ituri, aided by the government in Kinshasa, and there would be Lendu and Nande in charge in Ituri against the Hema. He said it was a direct attack on his Hema. He had had enough and he would wait no longer. The armed wing of the Hema's Union of Patriotic Congolese launched a surprise attack against Governor Molondo Lompondo and his smaller Ituri force. The next step would be to descend full force on the governor.

That was carrying things too far for Museveni. A few weeks later, in June 2002 Museveni invited Lubanga along with other Hema leaders to come to Kampala with a delegation of his men to talk about the escalating tensions in Ituri and explore ways to reach a peaceable solution. The delegation was graciously received, none of them suspecting it was a trap, and halfway through their stay Lubanga, along with select members of the delegation, was forcibly detained by Museveni's men, soon to be shipped off under armed guard to Kinshasa, where they were escorted by a military contingent to a prison. Perhaps it seemed to Museveni it was time to make amends with the young Kabila and his Congolese government in Kinshasa, and he would use the rebel Lubanga as a peace offering. Museveni may have thought this would dial down the overheated atmosphere in Ituri. But it did the opposite.

As soon as Lubanga was seized in Kampala, a few of his men slipped away from Kampala, and instead of returning to Ituri, they went straightaway to Rwanda. They knew, as everyone knew in that part of Africa, that Kagame in Rwanda would do anything to get a foothold in the DR Congo, and especially in Ituri, where the Ugandans were doing their business. Kagame had allied in the past with Museveni and the Ugandans, but Kagame would do anything – befriend or betray, it did not matter – and he did not care about the Hema or the Lendu or anyone else. He wanted land and minerals and power. Once Kagame was involved, things would become worse in Ituri, and it would not be long before Rwanda was airlifting heavy artillery and trainers for the Hema training camps outside of Bunia. Fighting would soon begin in earnest. And it made no difference where Lubanga was.

Governor Molondo Lompondo was new on the job when I arrived for a first visit back in April 2002. His fatigues were pressed, his shoes were un-scuffed, he wore heavy rimmed glasses, strictly functional and military issue, with no pretence to impress. He was a soldier through and through. His assignment was to govern as much as possible, contain the unrest in the region and provide services for those in need. With a shrug of his shoulder, he had shown me the folly of the assignment, as if the things he was doing and could do were really of no consequence. But he was a soldier. What about the Hema – could he contain them? He laughed. It was not the Hema he was worried about, though they were a threat. The Ugandans made things impossible. There would never be a government as long as the Ugandans were there, he said. They used Lubanga for their purposes, and when he became a liability, they shipped him off to Kinshasa. And now there were the Rwandans who would certainly use Lubanga, though he was not sure how at that point.

The governor knew then he could not maintain an army, even the small one he had, without financing, and the Ugandans controlled everything. There are villages that have nothing, he said in exasperation, their cattle seized by Ugandans and their farms destroyed, and we have international NGOs to help them with supplies. But the internationals have to pay exorbitant sums to Ugandan officers to use their trucks, and even if the NGOs paid what the Ugandans wanted and loaded the trucks themselves, the supplies were just as likely to disappear. Look here. He showed me piles of documents arrayed in a row on a table in an adjacent room and pulled one from the row labelled "préfinancement." Here were documents describing how the revenues that should have been collected by his border posts for import and export levies were documented but never paid by the Ugandans. They just took their stolen goods through the border posts with fraudulent documents saying they had already paid. His office had done a study. There was no money coming in. His small army was an army of volunteers living off pillaging and the pittance he had from Kinshasa. They would never stand up to Lubanga and the Hema, much less their masters from Uganda and now Rwanda.

"Tell that to the Security Council," he had said and thanked me for coming. I said I looked forward to meeting again in a couple of months.

"That might not be soon enough."

⁓

Three months had passed since that visit.

The mood of the Senegalese commander turned even darker as we approached the Governor's Office through a labyrinth of back roads. The drive was all evasive action. There had been killings and there would be more. The commander's main concern was keeping his men from getting hurt, and now he had to chauffeur a visitor under orders from his superiors through dangerous streets to meet with the most wanted man in the region. Not his job, he mumbled in French.

"Here," he said, "put this on. Wear a vest when you're with us. What you do after that is your business."

The Kenyan was back in the driver's seat, the Swede in the back.

He briefed us as if we were entering a battle zone. Do not get out of the car. Take cover only when advised. In case of gunfire, car enters avoidance mode.

Armed men in military gear were engaged in manoeuvres in the adjacent open field. As we came to a stop, the governor himself came out and stood on the veranda.

I was instructed not to leave the vehicle. The Senegalese pulled a cell phone from his shirt pocket.

"Here. You get in a tight spot, give us a call. We'll come if we can. Number's on it."

I thanked him.

"One thing if I were you. Be out at the airport in the morning and see if there's a plane coming through. Finish up your mission quick. That'd put you on the safe side."

I moved to get out of the car.

"Wait, they are motioning for us to come to the other side of the building. Where there's more cover."

A small army of the governor's bodyguards had gathered in the back courtyard, maybe a dozen of them where there were pickups with submachine guns mounted in the back.

"Before you go."

"What?"

"Be careful, my friend."

Things had changed since I had seen him last. The governor was decked now in rumpled unwashed green fatigues, flanked by his five-man personal guard. I was escorted from the back courtyard into his office. He waved me in. I almost did not recognize the man I had met and liked before. He was agitated. He looked a mess, with his military issue glasses cockeyed on his face. But he was still Kabila's man on the ground and he spoke with the measured cadence of a thoughtful officer, in contrast to the haggard men around him fresh from the front, wild-eyed, gripping their weapons. He asked me graciously about my family.

"Vous avez de la chance," he said with an ironic grin. "You find me alive."

"Indeed."

"You've been warned?"

"Warned?"

He paused a moment. "Something *pernicieux* has possessed this place, something without humanity. Have you seen the child soldiers? Lubanga's child soldiers?"

He motioned for me to sit down.

"No, I am quite serious. Have you seen the children? Have you seen Mandro, where they train them, and do you know who is training them? *Écoutez.* A month ago, a contingent of our men fifty strong assembled here before dawn and drove the twelve kilometres to the Mandro camp, where we joined another contingent who had gone on foot during the night and we entered the camp at daylight. Surprised them. There were caches of weapons in three stores, more weapons than you would imagine. They were Russian, imported through Uganda. Dropped in the forests a few kilometres from the camp. And who was using them? Boys and girls, some of them nine years old sent to the camp by their parents, Hema parents taking their children from school and giving them to Lubanga to kill and be killed."

He had a report on the arms observed at the training camp on his spare wooden desk. He picked it up and dropped it back down.

"We saw who was training them. Rwandans. And we know them. Here in Ituri. They are working for Lubanga. And there are always Ugandans somewhere with the Hema, even while he is in prison in Kinshasa. You know by now the Ugandans do as they wish. We cannot stand up to them, not with our small army of men, and yet we are still here. These men are death squads. We know them and we have told your United Nations, but they do nothing."

"The UN peacekeepers have abandoned us." He left to peer out the window onto the courtyard. "Where are they? Didn't wait for you? I don't see them."

"Returned to their base."

"Of course."

He picked up the report again. "I know why you are here and I thank you. You know about the Ugandans. Lubanga means nothing. He is just a dirty animal kicked around by his paymasters, but he is a dangerous animal. He will not be in Kinshasa long. He will return. Please my dear friend, take my Hilux sitting outside with the driver and drive to the border, not too far from here at Aru, and you will see the trucks belonging to the big Hema families, and you will inspect them, see they are full of valuable commodities for the Ugandans. Some perhaps for the Rwandans. Tell me what you see. No, do not tell me. Tell your friends at the UN. And they will know why the Ugandans have been dropping weapons in the forests outside of Mandro. And they will know why the Rwandans are happy to do the same. When you see them, you will know why Thomas Lubanga is a dangerous man. He wants everything, and he thinks his old friends from Kampala and his new friends from Kigali will help him."

"And you have documents?"

"I do, I do. *Regardez.*" He thumbed through another report. "Diamonds. You know, General Salim, half-brother to Museveni, has his eyes on diamonds and gold. That's well known. Here, look. Our study commission spent a week at the borders in Rutshuru, Butembo, and Mahagi and counted fifteen truckloads of wood a week from Mahagi, Mambasa, Dhera, each with thirty cubic metres. There were three truckloads of cattle stolen from local herders and skins taken from butchers. 3,000 skins last year."

"Rutshuru and Butembo and Mahagi, everywhere and my men at the customs would have stopped them, but they receive handsome favours to let things through. Lubanga's men have trucks that take everything across the border and return with petrol and soap and more. They have taken full control of our economy. We are under siege. One day it is cattle, another it is timber, then elephant tusks and monkey meat to sell to the Chinese, and the diamonds that come all the way from Kisangani. And gold. Bunia is famous for its gold. *Voici, prends-le,*" he said. "Take it with you."

He was weary. He straightened his thick black glasses. The room reeked of his fatigue, the scent of gunpowder, the exertion of his men, and the manioc boiling over an open fire in the courtyard.

He threw his hands in the air. "These Hema people would be nothing without the backing of the Ugandans, but they have it, and now there are the Rwandans and we are at their mercy. Everyone in Ituri is at their mercy. Our soldiers are country boys. They know the *mapanga*. That's what they know and they are strong boys, but the Hema have big weapons, grenade launchers. *Bon Dieu*, grenade launchers against our machetes. We need help and Kinshasa is the only one to give it to us. They don't."

A shot was fired and his personal guards turned around. Two of them left the room. The governor and I spoke for an hour about his career that spanned decades of turbulence in Congolese politics. The shots continued sporadically, though judging by his demeanour they were random firings of little consequence. Lunch was presented in a large porcelain bowl. I declined and we both stood up to see if the blue helmets had returned. They had not. I said I would take my chances.

chapter 3

Under Siege

I gathered my notebook and stepped outside.

The red-brown road from the Governor's Office into town was strangely deserted. There were usually families moving back and forth between villages and Congolese towns. Not a single woman bearing a water vessel with children in tow. Closer to town it was even more quiet. I began to worry.

Signs of war were everywhere. Buildings were cratered with bullet holes no one had bothered to repair. There were a few young men in fatigues sauntering in the streets nonchalantly waving their weapons about, marching in cadence, as if on a military lark, with no one in command. There were no customers at the restaurant Le Hellenique, which had been Bunia's meeting place for decades where the ever-present Sphinx-like owner, Mr Erkil, could usually be seen taking his espresso on the patio. Today he was hunched over, glancing occasionally into the street from his dark table inside. The main avenue in front of Le Hellenique had once been paved with the profits of the goldfields around Mongbwalu and beyond, not far from Bunia, and now with the state-owned gold-mining firm in the hands of Ugandans, the old asphalt on the streets had crumbled to pieces, leaving cavernous ruts.

Storefronts were boarded up. To my left, beyond the round-about, there had been two shops kept by Asians, and I was curious what had become of them since, even three months ago, their inventory suffered from the growing disorder, and I remembered the shopkeepers sitting disconsolately in their corners presiding over purchases of soap and matches and quarter litres of kerosene. The more costly items like plastic dinnerware and dental products were buried under dust from languishing on the shelves. I went towards the shops.

I found myself standing under a sign for a radio station inexplicably named TV 5. A few young people were working inside, and this was strange for a town nearly deserted. A young man emerged from a side street, hurrying by me as though fleeing an oncoming storm. I looked around and saw nothing. Another man came, also hurrying. A pause. Then another running at breakneck speed. There was a sudden commotion from the side street, the sound of shuffling boots, and it was only later I realized the boots I was hearing were many sizes too big for the feet of the children who wore them, sliding along the ground and turning the corner along the stretch of the main avenue where I stood.

I crossed the street and slipped into the shadows of a building set back from the street. The boy soldiers were on the move, heavily weighed down by their weapons and propelled somehow by war cries in an upper register. As I moved cautiously down the street away from them, away from the TV 5 storefront, someone peered from the doorway and suddenly bolted down the street. The boys opened fire. With a loud cry, the gang set off in chase. They stopped only to empty their magazines, some firing at the TV 5 sign and some at the person running down the street, and all with no one in command, no apparent reason or plan. I had no time to assess the situation. The person running from the place disappeared, scrambling in desperate fury, and for a moment I was relieved. Then another figure emerged from the building and a new blast of gunfire went up behind me.

What I saw in those few moments has stayed with me ever since. There was the grenade launcher that one of the boys pointed at the building. And when the grenade hit, it exploded with debris and concrete shards skimming in all directions. I did not see anyone hurt, but I did see the weapons, and I saw the boys behind them. They had stopped for a moment in front of the building to assess the situation, or because they were confused, or because whoever was guiding them was slow on the uptake, or because they were too busy firing their weapons that took the full concentration of twelve-year-olds. I have no idea if this was how old they were exactly, but I do know that young African boys at that age before puberty have a cherubic wide-eyed look like these boys, and I do remember thinking they were holding the guns at their waist because they seemed to lack the strength to hold them for any length of time against their shoulder. They pulled the trigger and had to struggle to hold on as it kicked back, nearly knocking them over.

I was not sure what to do, whether to run or stay in the shadows. They had not noticed me, or so it seemed, since they were in such a foment from the noise and flying debris. All the while there were bursts of weapons helter-skelter in all directions. In those few moments I saw how young they were, how utterly absurd it was for these boys who were only a few years older than my own young son to be running from one place to another, firing lethal bullets in random bursts.

However nonsensical it is for grown men to use destructive weapons, they usually do it in all seriousness with a sense of purpose. And even if the purpose is unforgivably callous, they do it with a gravity that commits them to the awful consequences. Not these little fellows. There was no purpose. They were just doing it, just jumping around flat-out on some kind of tear that added to the distraction of their youth. And like boys handling big machines, everything was taking place in an uproar. It is a terrible waste when men inflict such damage on each other, and yet how incomparably more wasteful it is when, in the hands of these young boys, it was for no more than the rip and fury of it all. The boys were waving their guns about as if they were at a birthday party.

Suddenly, they appeared to turn in my direction. I wrapped the small satchel carrying notebooks and the phone around my neck and dashed along the road, holding to the edges in the cover of the trees, though they provided feeble cover. I would have made an easy target for anyone with decent aim. I could only hope my darting here and there under the trees was as random as the boys' shooting, or they saw no need to concentrate on this foreigner in full flight. There was no whizzing of bullets. There were no explosions anywhere nearby. I could hear loud explosions coming from where I had been. I ran past a few houses that looked unwelcoming and then up an incline to where the road levelled off beneath a canopy of trees until I reached a junction, and on the corner to the left was a house with a boy standing outside peering curiously down the road. There was a fence. I rounded the corner, found a driveway, and ran pell-mell towards a door.

The man's face behind the door was unforgettable. He smiled, half in pity and half to counter my own expression of distress with a genuine understanding. He was thirty-five or forty, portly, with a rotund face and wire-rimmed glasses that gave him the appearance of a person in charge. The place looked like an office. Desks with papers lined the walls. There were logbooks, straight-back chairs and oddments of paper spilling out of accordion folders. It might have been a busy management section for a small service agency, except there was no one there. Gesturing with both hands, the man motioned for me to stay below the windows since the house was concrete and we were safe as long as we stayed low. Then he quietly guided me into another room where he sat me down on cushions placed along the floor next to a walkie-talkie and a radio crackling in Swahili.

"Shh," he said. "Were you in town?"

I nodded.

"How bad is it?"

I threw my hands in the air.

"Who are you with?"

"UN."

He rolled his eyes. "Goma? Kinshasa?"

"New York."

He rolled his eyes again. "Where's your protection? Where are your peacekeepers?"

"I was at the governor's. The peacekeepers didn't stay."

"Can you call them?"

I showed him the cell phone they had given me. I put it down beside me and looked around, not sure whether to blubber or chuckle.

He remained sitting next to me quietly and with a reassuring expression. This was nothing new to him. If he was here, in the midst of this commotion, it would have to be because he had a reason, a benevolent one, and my guess was he was heading an NGO. Somewhere in my satchel I had a list of NGOs to meet but could not make my fingers find the list. That would have to wait. He gestured again, down, down, stay down. My hands were shaking.

He motioned for me to go ahead and call. "Let them know where you are at least. They won't come get you. Just tell them and we stay where we are. Hopefully the boy soldiers don't get up this far."

He extended his hand with the phone, smiling.

"One thing, my friend. There's no hurry. You're safe. Those little guys are high on drugs and when they calm down they will go back to the school building where Lubanga's men keep them, and they'll be off the streets and asleep till tomorrow morning. They are just kids. You won't find them about the town."

"Your friends can come, just not here."

He read the question in my face.

"Look, it's the UN. You're the UN. The United Nations points fingers at the Ugandans and calls them criminals. Which they are and we know it, but we live with them. And as far as Lubanga is concerned, the UN is all for keeping him imprisoned in Kinshasa. He is the king of the Hema in Ituri, and we have to live with this guy. Is the UN going to stand up for us when it comes to Lubanga or the Ugandans? Not at all. The few blue helmets who are here stay in their base camp down towards the market and go for a ride two or three times a day in their white cars. And if they can't help us, then why should we take the chance to help them or even be seen with them?"

He shrugged and turned to the crackle on the radios and finally made contact with the UN radio room.

He made tea on a portable gas burner and opened a can of sardines.

He was from Goma. He had come two months before, after UNICEF found the child soldiers sent by Lubanga to Uganda for training at Kyankwanzi and Jinja and began sending them back. It had been two years ago in August when Museveni agreed to train 700 soldiers for Lubanga's own forces, and 159 of them were children. He was receiving those children as they returned.

"Thirty-four in the first group. Two girls. We look for their families and try to help them return home, which is hard, after the kids are used to living in training camps like little animals."

"You've seen them? Lubanga's kids?"

"They belong to Floribert Kisembo, in charge since Lubanga's in prison. And this guy knows it's against international law, but he likes the kids because they don't know what they're doing, and the parents won't do anything. Some actually give their kids to Lubanga. Take them out of school and put them into the army of the Union des Patriotes Congolaises, the Hema group."

"Parents do that?"

"Not all. Others get taken. Kisembo's men might march into a school and stand the kids up and anyone they think is older than eleven years old they put in a truck to Mandro or some other camp, and that's it. They fight. You saw them."

"That's it?"

"Some escape and run home and hide out, but if the commander hears about them, they go after them, and they've been known to kill them. We might get some of them if their parents don't stop them from getting help here."

He poured the tea over two cups half-filled with tea leaves and powdered creamer that clumped and curdled. His spoon clicked loudly in the empty room.

"The Hema have little mercy for the kids and less for anyone like our group to help them. They'd rather have us out of the way, and the same goes for other NGOs or anybody from the outside, and that's the United Nations too. They don't like outsiders looking around."

I nodded.

"That is what the Red Cross people were doing, working around the camps and making reports. And you know what happened."

This was a sensitive matter and had hovered over Ituri like a dangerous shadow for the last three months. Six workers for the International Red Cross were returning to Bunia from Fataki through Hema territory in the early afternoon, along a straight stretch in the road past a forested area, when five men stopped them – they must have known they were coming – got them out of their two cars and hacked them to death with machetes. They were laid one by one in a row on the road, four Congolese and two internationals, and the cars were set on fire. The way the bodies had been mutilated, splayed and displayed on the roadway and the cars left charred made it clear it was a murder with a message: foreigners with good intentions better watch their backs in Hema territory. There followed charades of investigation. Thomas Lubanga showed up two days later with his gang of Ugandan soldiers and made a display of expressing regrets and taking officious stock of what seemed to have happened. Witnesses were brought forward, some things were written down by police and the Ugandans, and these reports made their way into the hands of Human Rights Watch. Some days later a contingent of Ugandan soldiers returned to the site, rounded up people in the surrounding villages who might have seen or said something, and killed them all. They called it a "clean-up" exercise.[1]

After that, little more was said, though week by week and piece by piece information about the murder filtered out via the bush telegraph into the offices of activist NGOs and anyone else who would listen. It had been planned. The Hema high command were warning the International Red Cross and anyone else that they were on high alert for anyone interfering with what they were doing in Ituri.

Two witnesses to what happened eventually made contact with the Red Cross and named the culprits, two Ugandan soldiers and three Hema extremists. The Red Cross demanded these five be brought in for questioning, but it never happened. Instead, the Ugandans found a poor, unbalanced Lendu fellow who admitted to the murder and was punished with fanfare.

The NGOs took cover after that, and my friend said from then on he was especially careful. He carried his radio everywhere. The Hema might have wanted to keep foreigners out of their affairs, but after the Red Cross murders, investigators came all the way from Geneva, and there were the Human Rights Watch investigators and reporters from Nairobi, and instead of embargoing news about Ituri's growing chaos, the incident turned Ituri into a market for horror stories. Oxfam was sending out reports weekly. Bunia became a fishbowl of suspicions and dread.

"Watch yourself," he said.

We spent the rest of the afternoon on the floor, sometimes peeking above the windowsill. He found another can of sardines. In time the gunfire became intermittent. We checked in regularly with the peacekeepers, who stayed put until there was the calm of early evening as the children shuffled back. Only then the news came barking over the radio that the peacekeepers were on their way.

"Leave the house," he said. "Walk away from this place along the road that brought you here in the direction away from town, four to five minutes. They will find you on the side of the road."

~

The peacekeeper's base was a house on an undersized square of land surrounded by a high wall. The place might have housed four men comfortably, though it was quite a stretch for the eight peacekeepers who were living in the main house, plus guards and servants bunked in a small shed in a corner of the property. The threat of gunfire in the streets kept them sequestered behind the compound wall, and since many were in rooms shared with others with no refuge or privacy, most could be seen shuffling like haunts along the path that went halfway around the house and back again. They ate their meals together around a long table that stretched the length of the kitchen. And this night they talked about what they had seen on patrols, about the incident in front of TV 5, and about where the visitor would sleep.

The commander was sullen. "No place."

He looked around the table for confirmation. No one spoke.

"See for yourself," he said, turning in my direction. "Come along." He motioned for me to follow with his deputy.

The parlour was the only unoccupied space, but it was filled with radio equipment and the boxes it came in. There was a pantry full of food. The outside shed already had four occupants, and there were no rooms without two men at least and all their belongings.

"That's it," he said as we returned to the table. I happened then to spy a small door in the hallway opposite the entrance to the kitchen.

"What's that?"

"Unless you want to stay in a closet."

I turned the knob. It was a walk-in filled with luggage and jet-sam no one could find a place for, cleaning paraphernalia and fishing gear. It looked as if there might be room for a small army cot. I looked at the commander who cast an exasperated look at the men around the table and ordered two of them to clean the place out.

"Put up a cot."

Soon the hallway was filled with the oddments from the closet, leaving only a narrow passage.

"Luxury suite," he said. "In future if we are accommodating experts and watching out for them when they walk into a crossfire, we need facilities. See what I mean? You tell them. One night, my friend."

A diatribe ensued: yes, he had been informed the visitor was coming for a week, and he was also informed his men were to escort him to a border post. But he wanted to make one thing clear: Lubanga's forces were growing and the governor was slowly losing control, and when he did – which could be within the week – the commander was not going to protect anyone except his men and himself.

"This is not a suicide mission. Morning, first thing. One of you take mister expert to the travel offices where they have the planes in and out on the chalk boards, and get him on one, any one – Beni, Entebbe, Goma, Kinsangani – and check with the NGOs, see who's got people coming in and out, and then you go to the airport and stay there till something comes in."

The next day we visited a small agency in town where weekly flights were written in chalk on a board outside, each one a small one-plane operation. And when no one came to the door, we went around to the back where women were busy with chores and children. The owners were away, they said. Airplanes? Signboards? They shook their heads. The same at the other two agencies. Then the airport. We spent most of the day scanning the skies, but there were no planes in or out. That was enough to know there would be nothing coming into a town where gunfights broke out at least once a day and where one of the sides was decamped at the airfield.

The atmosphere inside the peacekeepers' compound was sour. The men, except for the commander, would have to accept their unwanted guest under the circumstances, even though every morning the Swede and I were obliged to make a ritual visit to the airport to discover, like the day before, there was nothing coming in or out. On the second day, I visited once again with Governor Lompondo Molondo, who sheepishly suggested in his kindly, matter-of-fact, military fashion that there could be an attack on his offices any day, and it was best to stay under the protection of the peacekeepers. Lubanga's forces were getting stronger. It was incomprehensible to him that Lubanga had been seized by Museveni himself and shipped to prison in Kinshasa while Museveni's troops continued to support Lubanga's army of Hemas. He was sorry. He wished he could help, and mostly he wished the UN could help him.

Word arrived from the Oxfam representative during the second day that local NGOs would assemble that night, and I was welcome to attend. The message included a special number to call when approaching the place. Invitees approached in the dark from different directions and conducted their business without lights, in quiet voices. And when everyone was there, we adjourned to a corner of a room surrounded by cloths hanging from the ceiling. The meeting opened with a note of remembrance for the six Red Cross workers. The situation, they said, was becoming grave. And please, they said, pointing to my notebook, inform anyone who will listen about us and about the catastrophe about to happen. If nothing is done, many will die. It is the Hema of course, the Hema High Council and the Hema businessmen. We know them, and you will know them if you stay long enough and see what they are doing. They are criminal. Behind them are the Ugandans and then there are the Rwandans. The Ugandans have despoiled this place. They care for no one, and they have allied with the worst of the Hema and pushed them and paid them to go to war. Even if you are Hema and do not want this, you have no choice.

Their voices were plaintive. We meet in darkness, they said, sometimes later than this. We want to continue our work, since villages are starving where the Ugandans have raided granaries and stolen cattle and left nothing. Thousands of cattle have been stolen. We supply clinics. We supply schools with books and lunches, and then there are the wounded and homeless everywhere. Their numbers are growing here in Bunia and throughout the region, mainly in the countryside. The problem is the Ugandans will not allow us to transport our supplies, health, food, books. We receive reports that cholera is spreading and that means thousands of children will die. They force us to use their trucks, and there are fees to pay. As of last week we pay also for a military escort, which would never be needed if they weren't here in the first place. Well, we could pay something, but our head office would never agree to give money to armed groups.

If they found us here together they would kill us. Like the Red Cross workers. No one would see it. It would just happen.

No one knows what we are telling you. We are in contact with our offices in Kinshasa and they write their offices in Europe, and still there is no help for us. Not really. No one dares come here.

They warned me be careful, the fighting would get worse.

The forays into town by the Hema child soldiers continued day by day, spreading fear and escalating the conflict beyond the real danger posed by the boys themselves and their pyrotechnics in the streets. The streets were mainly empty. We heard rumours that the Lendu and Ngiti, enemies of the Hema, had joined forces, and there might be others who would stand up to the Hema. Alarming reports of killings drifted in from different parts of Ituri. Agro Action Allemand, a German NGO, followed things closely, Oxfam's representative had their informants, and it was easy enough for me to meet Hema in the streets, caught in the jaws of Lubanga's ambition, since many of them had no appetite for the Hema jingoist rants, or the pressure put on families and their children to join the war. Now there was no choice. Lubanga had loosed a poison in Ituri society. There were moderate peaceable Hema who feared what would happen to them if they did not join the growing ranks of the UPC or if they did not send one of their boys or girls to the training camps and from there into the battlefields. There were families with mixed marriages, Hema and Lendu, who split up for their safety, each seeking refuge in their separate tribe's villages.

On the third day there was nothing at the airport, and we returned by late morning. The boy soldiers were already in the streets, and there was gunfire until early evening when it became quiet again, and it was then I felt safe to slip out the gate. There were more people in the streets, some older men for a stroll, some girls in what might have passed for finery, two priests in their vestments. I walked towards the market, keeping an eye on who was in front and who was behind, and particularly wary of the occasional boy in uniform when three of them sidled alongside and looked hard at me. They were armed. It was pitiful the look in their eyes, or more to the point, the lack of a look. There was nothing there, no curiosity, no spark of interest as there usually is among the ever-curious African children when they see a strange sight. No one shouted out the half-derisive, half-waggish word for white guy, *muzungu*. Their eyes were blank.

We walked together for a while. I looked off and on in their direction. Only once did we exchange glances, and it was when we were face-to-face that I felt as if something unpleasant was about to happen. At long last, they headed off in another direction.

Eight years later at Lubanga's trial in The Hague there was always the temptation for those of us in the public gallery to lean over the railing to get a glimpse through the glass at the face of Thomas Lubanga. The look was possible only for a few seconds before the guards in the gallery issued a stern warning to stay behind the brass rail and no gawking. Lubanga was seated in the far left-hand corner of the Trial Chamber, and in those few seconds I could see the same blank stare I had seen in the eyes of the three boys who had walked alongside me.

Two more days passed. We learned all United Nations flights in and out of Bunia had been cancelled. TMK had decided to bypass Bunia until further notice. The city was on its own as far as air traffic was concerned. My housemates' training as professional soldiers kept them collegial on the surface, even as the atmosphere in the compound turned increasingly rank. The closet where I burrowed myself had become my only refuge from the Senegalese commander who was more surly by the day with his barrage of accusations, while in town there were daily outbreaks of gunfire as the children paraded on their manoeuvres, rushing through the streets like furtive animals until they were tired and hungry and ready to trundle off in the late afternoon to their barracks. Only then was it safe to wander about, which I did to meet NGOs and concerned citizens who were willing to talk, and on one occasion I visited the governor again. It was then back to the compound and my refuge in the closet.

The sixth day began like the others. After breakfast, the men drifted into the courtyard to fire up their transistor radios. One of the men was to leave on R&R. He had brought his bags outside and kept his eyes on the sky, though he knew, as I knew, there would be no plane. He buried his face in his hands. A mangy dog scrabbled away in the dirt. Gunfire popped out of the neighbourhood behind us. The cook flung a bindle over his shoulder and slipped disconsolately into the street to a place he might find a few vegetables. We would have tomatoes with Spam tonight, a welcome change from the okra with Spam we had eaten the night before. Some of the men had taken to walking along a path around the house, around back of the garage, and staying close to the concrete walls, past the privy, and back to the courtyard. They walked for hours. When the commander had made morning radio contact with base in Kinshasa, he too slouched into the courtyard with nothing to say. An hour passed in brittle silence broken only by the clanging on the iron gate of a man selling charcoal from a wooden cart.

It was then we heard a droning sound, and all of us in the courtyard looked skyward, hoping against hope it would be the UN Beechcraft come to take the gloomy Kenyan for his R&R back to Goma, where he would find a ride to Kigali, and from there to Nairobi and his family. The droning grew louder, but the sound was of a different engine. It was approaching not from the west as it should have been if it was coming from Kinshasa, or from the south if it was coming from Goma, but the northeast from the Great Lakes, ploughing down low over the trees towards the Bunia strip. The Swedish officer assigned to my protection thrust his hand in his pocket for the Land Cruiser keys and motioned for me to get my things.

We honked, and the iron gate creaked open. We flew along the roadway that ran parallel to the airport, lurching from one side of the road to the other, past a defile of women carrying water and boys with sticks and hoops, swerving finally onto the airstrip in a cloud. A Toyota pickup was stationed behind the plane where two boys threw packages into the back of the plane. We parked the Cruiser at a safe distance. The cargo could have been arms, though no one seemed to care if we were there or not, not the two boys or the burly pilot in a jumpsuit standing by. These were not arms. The aroma was unmistakable once we got closer; it was fish, a plane-load of lake fish packed loosely in burlap bags reeking in the warm air. The plane was also unmistakable, a vintage Antonov, an oil-choked Russian flying truck. The belly of the plane was full of stinking tilapia, gobys, sleepers, and Nile perch, and supervising the operation was the Russian in his jumpsuit who cared nothing about gunfire or armed combat or boy soldiers or the Ugandan soldiers mustering out of their tents to inspect his cargo if they could get there in time. It was all in a day's work. He was a fish monger.

My Swedish friend tried his few words of Russian. The pilot shook his head. The Ugandan soldiers were beginning to organize at the far end of strip, though it was clear they would have to hurry, since the Russian had no intention of taking his time. Now was my chance. I pointed to my chest and then to the belly of the plane with a few words of Swahili. Expressionless, he waved one finger back and forth, appearing to say no. Not today. The last few burlap sacks were going in and the pilot moved to the back of the plane to push a few slippery sacks in place. I reached in my wallet and pulled out a fifty-dollar US bill, to which he responded by gesturing at my wallet, till it was clear he wanted to know if I had more. Two twenties later and I still was not sure, since the pilot was headed for the cockpit, until one of the boys nodded his head towards the mountain of fish and I sprang into the back of the plane as the pilot turned over the engine and retracted the ramp into place. It reeked. Thirty seconds later the Antonov was lumbering towards the end of the runway, revving the engines, churning its way down the strip into the air. It occurred to me that the smell of day-old fish in the sweltering heat was particularly agreeable.

chapter 4

From All Hell to The Hague

The Swedish peacekeeper said he'd phone if there was anything.

On the evening of 8 August, he called our office outside of Nairobi in a panic. The Ugandans were attacking the offices of Governor Molondo Lompondo. He had gone out for a look and seen people running in every direction. There had been skirmishes the day before, with Hema offensives in Lendu neighbourhoods and Lendu retaliating in Hema settlements. Deaths were multiplying by the hour, and armed combatants from all sides were running wild in the streets, some in uniforms, others in jeans, wielding knives, machetes, and clubs. The governor himself had gone to the airport earlier in the day to appeal to the Ugandan commander for calm. The commander rebuffed the governor and said he was under orders to remove him.

A brief raid on the Governor's Office in the evening gave him every reason to believe a full-scale assault was imminent.

I learned the next day that he was right, as dispatches came into our office from Kinshasa and New York. The governor should have departed the night before, but instead he stayed through the next day to lead his small contingent of poorly equipped young men against the seasoned Ugandans and the Hema armed groups, desperately trying to protect the non-Hema settlements. He knew he could not hold out but he did what he could, and it was only when the situation was hopeless, next day late in the afternoon, that he fled on foot, hiding here and there in houses and patches of trees. He should have received a medal.

Word spread quickly in and around Bunia that Ugandan armed contingents were leading the Hema charge against other ethnic groups, looting the homes and shops of anyone who was Lendu or Ngiti or Bira or Nande. Their victims ran wildly looking for some kind of shelter. Some who were under attack rushed to the UN compound, only to find that the peacekeepers could do little to protect them. Some fled to nearby settlements to hide from the Ugandan troops. Some were slaughtered on the spot. Some joined neighbourhood militias, though they were hardly a match for the combination of the Hema and their Ugandan allies. Governor Molondo Lompondo had never wielded much power, but he had been the only real local presence of the Congolese government. Now he was gone, and in his place was a renegade junta supported by a foreign government.

This all happened in forty-eight hours. The Hema militia under Lubanga's deputies and backed by the Ugandan army were firmly in power in Ituri.

The government in Kinshasa had to do something. It made little difference that they continued to hold Lubanga in prison. An entire block of the country was drifting into the hands of an absent warlord and his deputies manoeuvred by two neighbouring states. Kabila, the interim president, who had come to power after his father's assassination, would have to show the presence of the state, even if in name only. He requested that the minister of human rights, Mr Ntumba Luaba, fly to Ituri to assess the situation and dialogue with the Ugandans and their proxies, Lubanga's Hema High Council. Lubanga had only contempt for Kabila in Kinshasa, and one can imagine the scene when the minister arrived at the Hema training camp, where one of the big Hema personalities, Chief Kahwa Panga, had his headquarters. They were in their best fatigues. Chief Kahwa had put on his chiefly robes, and the minister was in his form-fitted *sapeur*-fashion Papa Wemba style. They were all smiles and swagger, knocking heads one side and another with Hema brothers. And yes, there was this matter of spilling blood and what are we to do?

He had come, said the minister, in the interests of peace. The Hema High Council listened dutifully, nodding and thanking their brothers who had come all the way from Kinshasa on a peacemaking mission. And when the minister was done, they said listen, the man for the job is our native son, Thomas Lubanga Dyilo. He is the one to calm curdling passions here. He is the one who can walk unharmed among the Lendu, the Ngiti, the Bira, and the Nande. And, *ecoutez* M. Le ministre, bring him from prison in Kinshasa and let us plan together. We shall work like brothers.

Minister Luaba thought about it. He may not have been all that sure just what Ituri's ethnic turmoil was all about. He might not have been briefed on why the Ugandans were there in Ituri or what had provoked the president of Uganda to seize Lubanga and send him to Kabila for safe-keeping. He certainly had no idea about the trap the Hema High Council were setting for him, because he stepped in with both feet when he said fine, he would return with their brother.

It was the most improbable of scenarios. On the morning of 26 August 2002, Minister Ntumba Luaba accompanied by Thomas Lubanga arrived at the Bunia airport from where they were escorted under heavily armed guard to the headquarters of Chief Kahwa once again. Again there were gifts for the minister, traditional dishes, and speeches and more declarations of brotherhood. They spoke of peace, a better life for their people. Chief Kahwa then motioned for the special guard of the Hema militia dressed in full battle gear to come forward. Thomas Lubanga, he said, would not be returning to Kinshasa and neither would the minister. The minister and his delegation were from that moment onward their hostages, and they would be kept at Camp Mandro under Hema armed guard until those Hema who remained in prison in Kinshasa were released and transported safely to Bunia.[1] Thomas Lubanga was back in charge.

Except this time was different. The ruse had been a diabolical success. Lubanga and his men had scored a coup and flush with success. Lubanga presided as if he had been chosen the ruler supreme. A new dogma spun out of his central command claiming the Hema of Ituri were the true Ituri citizens, *originaires* they called themselves, while the others were *non-originaires*. It was logical then for the *originaires* to claim land and property from those who were not true citizens, since the *non-originaires* were interlopers and inferior. It was a ruthless premise, because it followed that whoever was not Hema had no right to life, land, or property in Ituri. Lubanga did not wait long to act on this genocidal logic.

He prepared his fighting forces for combat. They went first to a gold-mining region, Mapanga, where the Lendu were trying to keep their foothold and the Hema armed forces led the charge. They conscripted anyone they could, Hema or not, to join them, promising them some of the spoils. And when the Lendu were defeated they turned on the non-Hema *non-originaires* who had helped them against the Lendu and slaughtered them all.

From there Lubanga directed his forces southward. This time they went after another ethnic group, the Ngiti, who until then had kept to themselves in the region. It was a massacre. The Hema forces went from one Ngiti house to the next in the small villages of the area and burned and raped and terrorized the population. The Ngiti had little recourse but to round up all the survivors and call on other members of their group to retaliate. Weeks later their attack on a Hema town was one of the bloodiest encounters of the Ituri wars.[2]

The Hema forces were now on the move. It wasn't long before they went after the prize, the biggest of the goldfields, Mongbwalu, where international companies had once worked their concessions and where the Hema forces and their Ugandan backers now wanted the goldfields to themselves. They murdered any gold-diggers who were not Hema, including the Lendu and Ngiti, and even the Nande, who were not diggers at all, since they were mainly traders. All were killed. The Pygmies from the forests who had come to work as diggers were killed. The farmers working the outlying fields were slaughtered for no apparent reason.

Lubanga's men frenzied on, naively supposing the ethnic foes would somehow disappear or be cowed under the onslaught. Raids and counter-raids led to one bloodbath after another until nearly the entire Ituri region was consumed by attacks and reprisals. Some were planned and might have passed for a military manoeuvre, and some were impromptu, more criminal than military.

None of the Hema offensives did much to subdue an ethnic adversary or send them into retreat, and they did even less to accord ruling privileges upon the Hema aggressors. In fact, the opposite occurred. The victims of Hema attacks struck back. From their neighbourhoods and beyond, they gathered all those able to fight and they defended themselves with machetes and farm tools when and where they could. They took their revenge, creating pockets of opposition throughout the region, one clash leading to another as the spread of violence picked up speed. Ngitis allied with the Lendu against the Hema, and the Hema and Bira against the Ngiti, and the Alur first with the Hema and then with the Lendu, with grievances multiplying and enmities expanding like a virus until the attacks and reprisals followed in rapid succession, engulfing everyone. After a while, there were only allies and enemies and nothing in between.

By March 2003 Ituri was soaked in blood. The only defence against Hema aggression was to go on the offensive against them. Sometimes a small tribal self-defence militia would strike out against the Hema on their own. Sometimes there were alliances. For the Hema there was no let-up; everyone was an enemy who did not embrace Lubanga's fervour for bringing all Ituri under the command of his Hema *originaires*. The assistant mayor of Bunia, a Hema himself, was seized and executed for sheltering Lendus. Ituri's most senior judge, with an impeccable reputation for impartiality, was imprisoned by the Hema command on suspicion of contact with Lendus. Anyone found trading with the Lendus was threatened or killed by Hema soldiers. Local NGOs were ransacked and closed down. International NGOs were under constant threat, and some left, remembering the killing of the Red Cross workers a few months earlier.

The violence was too pervasive for anyone to prevail. It would take something more, something more terrifying than guns and machetes and killing to strike fear in the heart of an enemy. Systematic rape was one thing. Reports from the war spoke of cannibalism. Hema commanders ordered their men to dissect and eat an enemy soldier in front of his compatriots. There even were rumours that enemy soldiers were forced to eat their own body parts.

Torture became as common as military manoeuvres. Human Rights Watch chronicled the accounts of torture in remarkable detail, publishing verbatim testimonies like that of a Lendu student suspected of having contact with the UN peacekeepers: "They kicked me with the butt of their guns. They undressed me. They dragged me to a shallow well and threw me in. They hit me with stones. I put my arms over my head. They asked what I was doing but they didn't let me answer. There were seven of us in a space of two square metres. It lasted for four days. The interrogation continued. They beat me with sticks. Then they forced me into the well again."[3]

Meanwhile, Museveni's men carried on, seizing gold and other precious metals, timber, and diamonds and shipping them to Kampala, conscripting Iturians of one group and another whenever it suited them. Everyone knew of their sordid presence by now and how they were abetting the violence in Ituri as a cover for their exploits; hints of horrors were leaking into the international press. In rare moments of remorse, some Ugandan officers even admitted their crimes publicly and apologized. Once again Museveni played the statesman to make a show of working for peace in Ituri by summoning to Kampala the political figures of the Ngiti and the Lendu and the Alur and the Hema, though it was obvious to everyone that it was too little and too late and it had to be either guile or naivety that led Museveni to think he could persuade anyone to seriously join in. He shamelessly branded his peace-building initiative Operation Safe Haven. It was as if an assembly of foxes had set up a peacekeeping mission inside a chicken run, hardly credible and bound to end in disaster. Still Museveni pressed shamelessly on in search of international redemption. On 6 March 2003, he ordered his armed forces to attack the Hema command controlling Bunia and run the leaders out of town, as if he were Bunia's protector against the Hema aggressors. It mattered little that the Hema were also his partners in crime.

Meanwhile, the Rwandans took Lubanga away to Kigali for temporary safekeeping; they knew, as everyone knew, how capricious Museveni was, how this was a cosmetic manoeuvre, how it would all blow over soon and how the Ugandan troops would return to exploiting Ituri's resources. As expected, the Ugandan troopers were gone in a week. The Rwandans reinstalled Lubanga as their man in Ituri. The United Nations hoped to extend the respite from fighting by sending in a large contingent of Uruguayan troops to keep things under control at the airport, but it made little difference, because once the Ugandans went back to their pillaging, the Hema command returned and the massacres started anew.

By now Ituri was an international disaster. It seemed Lubanga would never relinquish his campaign for supremacy, and the killings could go on indefinitely with the backing of Rwanda and the complicity of the Ugandans. This called for extreme measures.

UN Secretary General Kofi Annan appealed to the French government to assemble a multinational force to put an end to the Ituri conflict. The French agreed, and by the first week of June 2003 Operation Artemis was in place with a combination of French and European Union forces. There was nothing frivolous about Operation Artemis, as there had been with the Ugandans' Operation Safe Haven. Once installed in Bunia, the multinational force enforced a ban on weapons in Bunia that applied to all groups. When the force encountered any armed groups, whether Hema or Lendu or Ngiti or Nande defying the ban, there were real consequences. Operation Artemis meant business: armed groups remaining in Bunia had no choice but to leave for the countryside, and slowly over the summer of 2003 life in Bunia returned to something close to normal. A functioning economy resumed. Goods began to come in from the Middle East as before, and families could once again be seen walking the streets. Operation Artemis did what the Ugandans only pretended to do and what the United Nations had been unable to do. It gave the United Nations enough time to reinforce its peacekeepers in Ituri with troops from Nepal and India and Bangladesh.

The Ugandan forces kept their distance from the city of Bunia during Operation Artemis, still pretending as before that they were in Ituri in the interests of peace. The armed groups who remained left their stations around Bunia and shifted to the north towards Fataki and Mahagi, and Irumu to the south. None of the groups, Hema included, could pretend any longer to have any real power. As long as Operation Artemis was in place with its predominantly French soldiers and commanders, the French were in charge. It was a relief to the majority of the population, who were once again free to venture freely from their houses, do business if there was any business to do, leave their arms, and return to their farms. Not Lubanga, however. Lubanga now had another enemy to contend with: the French. He still aimed to subdue the Lendu and the Ngiti, but it was the French who stood in his way as long as Operation Artemis was around. He bided his time. And when Operation Artemis was replaced by the United Nations, it was no longer the French but the UN peacekeepers who were his adversary.[4]

Bunia and the surrounding areas were no longer war zones. Most of the protagonists, Lubanga excepted, seemed to accept that it was futile to continue the combat. As Operation Artemis came to an end, newer and larger contingents of UN peacekeepers came into Ituri. It was better for those who had taken up arms in the Ituri wars to accept Kabila's invitation to talk peace in Kinshasa. Lubanga agreed to join the others in Kinshasa in August 2003, though it was only for show, since he had no intention of giving up his designs for controlling Ituri. He kept his Hema army intact. He continued to make deals with the Rwandans to keep his men supplied with weapons and military advice, and it was well known while he was in Kinshasa supposedly talking peace that he was using his political leverage angling for political support to keep his power base in Ituri alive. Everyone knew Lubanga was maintaining his ties with the troublemaker Rwanda to wreak more havoc in Ituri.

President Kabila eventually placed Lubanga under house arrest.

Meanwhile, Lubanga's men continued to attack others in remote locations. The place was still awash with arms. There was little anyone could do, apart from the occasional disarmament program that gave compensation and training to members of armed groups still roaming the bush, in exchange for handing in their weapons. Small groups of renegade soldiers, Hema forces especially, remained sequestered in encampments distant from Bunia, preying on villagers and attacking anyone who tried to stop them. On one especially important occasion this included United Nations peacekeepers who happened upon Lubanga's men.

It happened in early 2005. A small contingent of armed men in rural Ituri were stopped by nine Bangladeshi peacekeepers under orders to rid the area of non-state armed elements. They ordered them to put down their weapons. Instead, the renegade soldiers opened fire and killed every one of the Bangladeshis. It was a turning point for the United Nations officials in the Democratic Republic of the Congo, who had had enough and who finally acted decisively: all renegade and rebel group leaders who continued to operate in Ituri – and this meant Hema and Lendu and Ngiti and Alur and Nande, all of them – would be tracked down and imprisoned. It was a shame that it took the deaths of nine peacekeepers to close off this chapter of Ituri's horrors, but it did, and the leaders were captured and placed in jail. Thomas Lubanga was shifted from house arrest in Kinshasa to a military prison.[5]

Most of those captured were kept in detention centres, and this is where they stayed. Thomas Lubanga was a special case. He had achieved global notoriety for his ruthlessness. His crimes had been so monstrous and his guilt so patent that of all the political criminals worldwide, the Office of the Prosecution at the International Criminal Court regarded Thomas Lubanga as obvious choice to stand trial in the first case of the International Criminal Court on charges of war crimes and crimes against humanity. Meanwhile Lubanga's men continued to flail away at the United Nations, firing on peacekeepers and their helicopters. The secretary general's special envoy in the DR Congo appealed to Lubanga to call his men off. Lubanga refused, adding to his reputation and to the prosecution's view that Lubanga was the right choice for the Court's inaugural trial. A final decision was made on 10 February 2006 with a warrant issued for his arrest on the charge of conscripting, enlisting, and using child soldiers under the age of fifteen. A month later on 16 March 2006 Lubanga was transferred to a prison outside of The Hague near the Court to await trial.

His transfer was a momentous passage in global affairs.

Legal experts, human rights advocates, and statesmen from around the world had finally arrived at a global consensus to punish crimes known to be so heinous they applied irrespective of the juridical convention of states and their separate dominions. This was universal jurisdiction, and nothing quite like it had existed before. There had never been a court able to prosecute individuals no matter where they came from, and now, with some exceptions, there was. Lubanga's passage christened the birth of a court with something close to universal coverage, and it was no small matter, because once it was acknowledged that there were crimes on which everyone agreed, all peoples from Albania to Zanzibar shared a collective identity on matters of international justice.

Now there was nowhere for Lubanga to hide, no jurisdictional loophole or sovereign state for his refuge. Ten years earlier, Lubanga might have slipped away from legal scrutiny or even come away with a post in the Congolese government. He might have retired to a safe location in his home province, as had the equally brutal leader, Augusto Pinochet of Chile, who had been pardoned by Chile's Parliament and protected from prosecution for crimes against his people. There would be no pardon for Lubanga. The Congolese government had accepted the Court's intervention in the Lubanga case as a rightful complement to its own competence in administering justice.

As he was ushered by security personnel from the prison in Kinshasa to the fortress of a jail near The Hague in Schevinengen, Thomas Lubanga might well have wondered, Why me? He might have assumed he could do as he wished in the woolly scrum of post-war Congolese politics, where power was power and some people had always died for others to rise. This was government African style. There were other politicians in the Democratic Republic of the Congo who had done what he had done, and he knew them, Etienne Tshisekedi for instance, a national figure who had been prime minister for a short while under Mobutu. In fact, Lubanga had worked on the man's political campaigns, and he knew Tshisekedi had done as much harm in defence of his own tribe, the Luba, as Lubanga had done in defence of his. Where was Tshisekedi now? He was still in politics. Then there was Mobutu. He had condoned ethnic cleansing to pull the political rug out from under Tshisekedi, and that was the least of his crimes. And at the end of his reign he was a leopard and a legend, not a criminal. As for Lubanga, he was being shovelled into a cell in a foreign land.

More deeply than any international body ever before, the International Criminal Court was now reaching into states like the DR Congo to end impunity where no international body had been able before.

It had been a long road to get to this point. After the Nuremberg and Tokyo trials there was a lot of discussion about creating a court of even greater scope than these two. At the time, it seemed only natural to imagine that something like these courts could do for all states what these two had done in Germany and Japan. Except that few states were interested. Everyone liked the lofty ideals of an international court, but few states were ready to accept a court with the right to hold their own governing practices in judgment. Hardly any notice was taken when the United Nations General Assembly created a committee with the portentous title of Progressive Development of International Law and Its Codification, or when this committee in turn put in place the International Law Commission. This International Law Commission worked hard, but it also laboured in obscurity, and the idea of an international court languished for fifty years.

For more than three centuries state sovereignty had been the unalterable global norm for states. State authorities could do whatever they wanted with their citizens. They could disembowel them or dispossess them if they felt inclined, and only those within the state could pass judgment, if they dared. The world at large might disapprove of what a state was doing inside its borders, but that meant little because within state boundaries state power was subject to no law other than its own, and that left a lot of room for abuse. States could do largely what they wanted, and it is little wonder that – as much as an international court appealed to visionary jurists – it appealed hardly at all to the political authorities of most states.

The end of the Cold War was the catalyst for a sea change.[6] As the two global protagonists withdrew from their strategic alliances around the world, the lid was removed from a string of trouble spots, which turned into political disasters. Few unstable troubled states had an interest in protecting their citizens and could just as easily become their citizens' worst enemy. There was the defiance of Saddam Hussein in Iraq followed by harsh sanctions that brought Iraq's people to the brink of starvation. Slobodan Milosevic butchered innocent people in Srebrenica and laughed at the international community for disapproving. Somalia became a notorious cauldron of political turmoil where no one was safe. Rwanda exploded with violence following a Tutsi-led coup d'état and a violent Hutu response that ended up a massacre that no one could stop. The Democratic Republic of the Congo erupted in a chaos of conflict that took over five million lives by the time it was over.

Tragedies accumulated. There was no end in sight at the end of the decade. The big question was how to respond to these political disasters as long as state sovereignty stood in the way or offered an excuse not to intervene. Secretary General Kofi Annan knew something had to be done, and in the year 2000 as he was writing his vision of the United Nations in the twenty-first century in a memorable paper, We the Peoples, he asked a simple question: "If humanitarian intervention is indeed an unacceptable assault on sovereignty, how should we respond to a Rwanda, to a Srebrenica – to gross and systematic violations of human rights that offend every precept of our common humanity?"[7] And there followed a felicitous answer, proposed by the Canadian Commission on Intervention and State Sovereignty: "the responsibility to protect." International bodies could and should intervene, and this was not just an option, it was a responsibility.

The idea of an international court that had lain dormant in the International Law Commission for so many years emerged as part of the answer. An international court would punish abusive politicians and deter those who had pretensions of becoming abusive. It would limit the prerogative of national leaders, warlords, and other perpetrators of crimes against humanity hiding behind the sovereignty principle. The idea of a world court that had been dormant for so long and that seemed so impracticable was now being discussed and seemed increasingly viable. If the General Assembly had called a meeting of states to discuss a world court in the 1980s, few would have thought it worthwhile to attend, but when the General Assembly proposed a Conference of Plenipotentiaries on the Establishment of an International Criminal Court in June 1998, the number of nation states who wanted to come exceeded all expectations.

As it turned out, more than 150 states sent delegations to that conference in Rome and they were joined by hundreds of international organizations. As the conference got underway, support for the court grew quite unexpectedly. African and Arab states took strong positions on human rights that in some instances overrode the more conservative European positions. The world was surprisingly ready. The charter for an international court, the Rome Statute, was approved by a landslide majority and advanced the idea towards the ratification stage. Again no one was sure. Senegal was the first to ratify in February 1999, followed by Trinidad and Tobago two months later, and over the next two years, state by state ratified until 11 April 2002, when the target number was reached. On that date a court to protect against human rights abuses had broken through the hard shell of state sovereignty, and while it might have been less noticed at the time, it was as extraordinary a moment as the birth of the United Nations fifty-eight years before.

chapter 5

Low-Hanging Fruit

There was nothing inherently wrong with the one and only charge against Lubanga, using children to fight, since it was clear Lubanga and his commanders had brought large numbers of young children into their ranks. The problem was that recruiting children was a relatively minor matter, given the full scope of the man's crimes.

The prosecutor had his reasons for keeping the charge to a minimum. Better for him to win a small prize than lose the first case altogether, since he knew well how the sharp contours of whatever evidence he might muster against Lubanga could become murky once the trial started. The judges would see first to proper procedures and stand firm for the protection of the accused, pushing evidence into corners where it could easily be dismissed or doubted. Even in the very early stages, during the pretrial hearing the proceedings careened from one procedural wrangle to the next, and with every query and every objection the hard assurances of Lubanga's guilt became softer. An aggressive defence would have little trouble convincing the Chamber that the prosecution's witnesses would say anything, even lie if they thought it would qualify them for a protection program and a trip out of Ituri. This was just the beginning. Charging Lubanga with conscripting children was thought to be safe, if not fully just, and it was better to place bets on what seemed a sure thing than stake the case on the more serious matters of genocide, torture, sexual enslavement, and other crimes against humanity, where standards of proof might be more difficult to satisfy. Lubanga was guilty of most of them,[1] but the charge of conscripting child soldiers was low-hanging fruit. Or so it seemed.

This is not to diminish the crime or the articles in the Rome Statute that name the recruitment of children a crime. Seizing children from school or from the street or forcing parents to give their children to a warlord's militia is perverse; children have no place in war. Few would disagree, and in the long history of war in the world, very few societies have been crass enough to train children to kill. Maybe the Spartans in ancient Greece and maybe the Janissaries who served the Ottomans in the thirteenth century, but the only children the Ottomans recruited were Christians and they never took them from their own Muslim faith, or any children, for that matter, for whom they had strong sympathies. Even the most militaristic of societies have stopped short of using children in war.

Genocide and rape, enslavement and torture are the crimes that attract the most serious attention. They are the acts so universally reprehensible that there are no contingent circumstances to mitigate their criminality. These were among Lubanga's prime strategies, but they were not included among the charges and as a consequence they rarely came up in the trial as the prosecutor struggled to pin down the charge of child soldiering. Everyone knew there was something wrong with this, they just did not say so. For better or worse, the prosecution held to the easy road for a conviction, and once the charge was laid and confirmed, the chief trial judge, a stickler for legal procedure, refused to listen to testimony about mass rapes or mass killings. He would make the prosecutor live with his earlier decision.

Crimes, like personae in a novel, have their temperaments. Some are exotic and rare – enslavement for instance, or the disappearance of persons – and one has to read their description carefully. These lurk in the shadows of history and are seen only on special occasions. War crimes are different, since so many are run-of-the-mill, like taking enemies hostage or torturing them or deliberately attacking civilians; they hardly need introduction. A very few are so heinous and heavy and rooted in historical abhorrence that when they are applied, they are applied with caution – genocide, for example.

Then there are crimes that have only recently come into the legal corpus. "Forced marriage" is one recently catalogued and used in the conviction of Sierra Leone commanders for taking bush wives during combat, holding young girls for their pleasure against their will. It is a version of sexual violence and one that should have been in the corpus long ago but had to wait for growing social awareness before it could get in. Finally there are the crimes of using children in war. They look easy enough to prove, since there may be lots of child soldiers around to testify, but they are too fresh for prosecutors to know much about them.[2] Before the 2006 conviction of the Revolutionary United Front soldiers in the Special Court for Sierra Leone, they had never been used in a courtroom.

There had been no mention of child soldiers in the Geneva Conventions of 1949. There was no mention of child soldiers in the United Nations Charter or the Universal Declaration of Human Rights. Nor any mention of using children in combat in the Charter of the International Military Tribunal at Nuremburg drafted at the end of the Second World War. The wars of the twentieth century were bound up with the affairs of states, with seizing states, mobilizing them, disabling them, and controlling them with flags waving in time to their noble pretensions, while national armies did their landings and bombings. And if, by the way, women were raped and children were mistreated, these less panoramic crimes did not stand out among matters of legal concern.

It was not until thirty years later that individual women and children attracted much notice in international law, and that was not until the character of war began to change, until war lost its virtue and fell into the hands of villains and warlords and was no longer the solemn duty of soldiers who fought for glory and returned home to regular jobs. Wars became a dirtier business once the protagonists were mainly opportunists like the young rebels on the eastern side of the Democratic Republic of the Congo whose interest in fighting is gain, not virtue. They are not heroes, only survivors, if indeed they survive. They are not fighting for a better life, for the only better life is to pillage a village and steal crops and chickens for a meal and a stay of their own difficult circumstances. The spoils of victory have far less to do with security or freedom than with the gruel and the cash from the week's manoeuvres.

These child soldiers are not so much soldiers as they are social orphans who know nothing about the conventions of war, the treatment of prisoners, or care for the injured. Or treatment of civilians, for that matter, since these are new wars in which civilians are targets of attack and preferred victims for the obvious reason that, unlike an enemy opponent who might counter with aggression of their own, civilians are easy prey. And it was not just boys among the soldiers, it was underage girls and nearly as many of them. The commonly held view that girl soldiers were little more than "camp followers" would have to change because they were far more; they cooked for the men, carried supplies, brought in provisions, did what the state would normally do to sustain a fighting force on the move. They ran messages from one site to another and served as army wives for commanders who in the end treated them with uncommon contempt.[3] War had become a business for rebels and governments alike, and using children made a dirty business even dirtier.

It took some years for all this to sink in among jurists. Using children in warfare entered the corpus of "soft" international law slowly.[4] Jurists saw it as a minor issue. In 1977 as additions were being made to the Geneva Conventions about protecting medical personnel or protecting civilians and their possessions or the treatment of prisoners, changes were also on the agenda for protecting children. In retrospect it seems to have been an afterthought: a provision was included that said parties to a conflict "shall take all feasible measures in order that children who have not attained the age of fifteen years do not take a direct part in hostilities."[5] That was not a very strong injunction and the drafters knew it. Some justification was needed, and the one given in the commentary is hardly compelling. It was that children brandishing rifles and machine guns, immature as they are, pose a danger to those around them; repeater rifles in the hands of kids could go off anywhere.

The truth is that, at the time, few commentators were in favour. Some called the provision that discouraged the recruitment of child soldiers a "shallow foundation" for a war crime. Others said it was unfair to impose an unconditional obligation on militias in this way because who could nay-say the heroic efforts of children in a war of liberation. Still others preferred to concentrate on health care and education for kids and less on the more particular matter of kids joining or being pressed into fighting armies.

The Convention of the Rights of the Child adopted in November 1989 might have moved the law a step closer to keeping children out of war. It was approved with customary pomp; in the convention there was even an article imposing on states the obligation to "refrain from recruiting any person who has not attained the age of fifteen years into their armed forces." But it was the obligation of states and not rebel groups to refrain from using child soldiers, when in fact it was mainly rebel groups who were doing it. That made the convention somewhat beside the point, especially because the world would soon hear about the boy soldiers of Sierra Leone and the *kadogos* (little soldiers) of the Congo. The number of child soldiers would soon increase dramatically, and if this Convention on the Rights of the Child was going to protect children from armed conflict, it needed something more sturdy.

It needed something more than optional protocols or amended conventions.

During a meeting of the Committee for the Convention on the Rights of the Child, it was proposed that a study on the impact of war on children be carried out. No one objected. Then someone suggested it be headed by Graca Machel from Mozambique. It is doubtful that the committee realized at the time that Machel would bring more attention to the matter of children in war than all of the declarations or conventions put together. She was a game-changer.

Graca Machel is from a backwater province in Mozambique; her father was a farmer, and when the farm did not do well, like so many others in his day, he went off to work in the mines in South Africa. She was a bright student, and after a rural education with Methodist missionaries, she was chosen for education in Lisbon where she studied German and wrote a thesis on German philosophy. She returned to Mozambique an educated woman, joined FRELIMO, the Mozambique liberation movement and, in time, married its leader, Samora Machel. President Machel died tragically in an airplane crash a few years later and Graca Machel would later become the third wife of Nelson Mandela. She had a destiny. She had championed education, had become a symbol of reconciliation and national unity in her country, and now she was the choice of the General Assembly to lead the study on the impact of war on children. The details of the report she submitted were shocking in their own right, but what was more memorable was the imprint of her convictions. When the report came out in 1996, it became a rallying cry to place children in war prominently on the international stage.[6] The secretary general created a new department to deal with the report's recommendations. Canada hosted a global conference in 2000 devoted to the matter, and largely as a result of Machel's influence, the Convention on the Rights of the Child came to have a liturgical quality as the General Assembly adopted an addition to the Convention, an optional protocol that this time made the crime of recruiting child soldiers far tougher. She made the world sit upright and take the matter seriously. And in the space of ten years, child soldiers went from the shadows to the spotlight.

In the lead up to the Lubanga trial, what the prosecutor anticipated, and doubtless what attracted him as he settled finally on the one and only charge of using child soldiers, was that the charge might have been thin but it was new and urgent and would attract public attention. For once jurists and politicians and journalists cared about little boys and girls carrying guns through the bush and were horrified at how many there were and how they were drugged and told to kill other children if they wanted to live. Putting child soldiers on the front line of the case would put the trial on the front pages.

But there were drawbacks. When Lubanga was charged, the crime of which he was accused had star power, but the prosecution had too little experience in the trenches of a courtroom, where the legal footing would get slippery. Outside the courtroom there was an even larger problem: from the vantage point of everyone who cared, charging Lubanga with this one crime seemed grossly inadequate, considering all he had done.

~

"All rise."

The pretrial proceedings opened on 20 March 2006. The arrest warrant had been delivered. Thomas Lubanga had been remanded four days earlier from Kinshasa into the custody of officers of the Court in The Hague. From early afternoon, the pretrial chamber bustled with activity, the gallery was full of onlookers, legal tourists, humanitarians, law students, and curious bystanders as the court officer portentously announced the arrival of Judge Claude Jorda.

Judge Jorda was a veteran of the International Criminal Trials for Yugoslavia. He entered the Chamber robed in black, a grandfatherly scholar of a man with a humble bearing, though he was far from a retiring elder. He was on a mission. He harboured a profound impatience with the legal machinations in trials of this sort that held war crime trials hostage to procedure and bogged them down. It was egregious, he was known to say, how the Rwanda and Yugoslavia trials were sadly prolonged. In the International Criminal Tribunal for Yugoslavia he had personally endured interminable stays and delays that gave war criminals a reprieve while his own patience wore thin. It was a problem and he had made known his solution: the pretrial. If there were procedural issues, his advice to the drafters of the Rome Statute was to deal with them before the trial started in something akin to a hearing that he dubbed a pretrial. The idea had struck a chord and made its way into the procedures for the new International Criminal Court. Long trials, he argued, were a scourge: eighteen months was the maximum and any longer was a disservice to the law and to the accused. No more than four months for the pretrial, he said, twelve months for the trial proper, and the trial would be over in a year and a half.

Judge Jorda took the floor after a few initial words: "I would now like to ask Mr Thomas Lubanga Dyilo to stand and to answer a number of questions to ascertain his identity. These are basic questions. We would like you to confirm your name, your date of birth, and your profession." Observers in the public gallery craned their necks to have a better look.

Thomas Lubanga: "My name is Thomas Lubanga Dyilo. I was born on the twenty-ninth of December, 1960 in Jiba in the Democratic Republic of the Congo. I am a politician by profession."

The judge replied, "I'm afraid I didn't hear every word you said. You said you are a politician? Do you have anything to add at this time?"

Thomas Lubanga Dyilo declined to answer.

"Very well. Thank you. You may be seated."

The judge got right to work seeking agreements from both sides on protection of witnesses, on conditions of Lubanga's detention and on evidence disclosure. He wanted things to move quickly. But they didn't. The defence wanted documents the prosecution had promised the United Nations to keep confidential, and the defence cried foul. Turning over the documents would take time. The prosecution gave some, not all. The judge cut short long disquisitions from both sides. Still there were more requests for documents, motions for this and that, and delays. Weeks turned to months and the frustration of Judge Jorda grew as their target of concluding in four months receded, first slipping by one month and then two and four until September, and still procedural issues were pending while there was still no confirmation of the charges. These were the early warning signs of the creep of legal tedium that would plague the trial throughout.

Judge Jorda soon realized to his chagrin that his mission was impossible. As long as celebrity lawyers were playing to a world stage, there was nothing he could do to keep the courtroom on script.

Meanwhile, the prosecutor was worriedly watching the pretrial veer to one side and another, away from its simple function of confirming the charges. Matters would only be worse once the real trial started. There had been pressure on the prosecutor to broaden the charges, and the truth was he was sorely tempted, for the charges, he knew, were the elephant in the room. There had been little mention about the one minor charge inside the Chamber but there did not have to be: it was on everyone's mind how the charge, being so light, did a disservice to the Court and its reputation. You could hear it in the corridors. You could hear it from the powerful civil societies, Human Rights Watch and the Federation international des ligues des droits de l'homme. The prosecutor was torn between two poles, whether to remain true to what he knew was the right thing, that is to open the charges up to a host of crimes; or whether he should err, self-servingly perhaps, on the safe side and keep things simple since by his reckoning, no one could gainsay Lubanga's use of child soldiers with the myriad testimonies and witnesses and reliable reports. The pretrial delays were a sign that broadening the charges might muddy his chances.

It was a dilemma for the prosecutor. His experience in Uganda a few years earlier was undoubtedly on his mind. In 2005 the prosecutor had asked Uganda's President Museveni to refer the case of Joseph Kony and his Lord's Resistance Army to the Court. The Lord's Resistance Army was a fearsome group that had enslaved children and terrorized the population in Northern Uganda. President Museveni agreed at first and it all seemed simple enough until Museveni realized the investigations would end up showing his own national army to be as guilty of atrocities as the Lord's Resistance Army, and then he began to waffle. Trying Kony and his men for crimes against humanity while turning a blind eye to the crimes of Museveni's men would not look good. What made things even more complicated was that the Court did not have the means to arrest Kony and his men. In the end, the case unravelled.

Better now to keep things simple in the Lubanga case. Make sure the Congolese government was on board and keep the charges light enough to guarantee a conviction. The prosecutor knew the right thing to do was to broaden the charges, but if the pretrial was any indication of the gantlet ahead of him, there was reason to worry.

It was not an easy decision and even once the decision was made, he had his doubts. He kept the prosecution's five investigators on the ground in Ituri chronicling events and gathering evidence for rape and murder, just in case the Office of the Prosecution needed the ammunition to broaden the charges. He kept them there in spite of the fact that they laboured under the threatening eye of the chiefly Hema families who had little patience with anyone collecting evidence against their leader. They would also stay in spite of the upcoming Congolese elections of 2006 that had officials at the Court nervous about security.

He kept them there until serious concerns emerged about their safety. For anyone who knew the place and its politics, things were probably not as serious as the Court imagined. But all the talk did offer a fine excuse for finally settling the matter of the charges, since pulling out the investigators would end the investigation into the bigger crimes. The charge would remain limited to the recruitment of child soldiers. The prospects of charging Lubanga with murder and rape had been daunting from the start and now, with the ongoing contortions inside the pretrial chamber, they were that much more so. There was no guarantee the trial proper would be any less convulsed by courtroom strategies than the pretrial was. There would be disputes over how much of the prosecution's evidence would have to be disclosed and whether the NGO reports on the crimes – those of Human Rights Watch, for instance – could be believed. But the prosecutor had taken his own measure of what he had seen and what was before him and concluded it was better, if less honourable, to settle finally on a lesser charge.

On 28 June, the prosecutor announced to the pretrial chamber that he was suspending his office's Ituri investigations into the case against Thomas Lubanga. The reaction was blunt. A group of human rights organizations, addressing the prosecutor, wrote:

We are disappointed that two years of investigation by your office has not yielded a broader range of charges against Mr Lubanga. Charging those responsible for the most serious crimes committed in Ituri – including, but not limited to Mr Lubanga – with representative crimes for which there is a strong evidentiary basis is crucial for the victims of these crimes and for ending the culture of impunity in the DRC and in the Great Lakes Region. We believe that the failure to include additional charges in the case against Mr Lubanga could undercut the credibility of the ICC in the DRC. Moreover, the narrow scope of the current charges may result in severely limiting victims' participation in the first proceedings before the ICC. This could negatively impact on the right of victims to reparations. We believe that you, as the prosecutor, must send a clear signal to the victims in Ituri and the people of the DRC that those who perpetrate crimes such as rape, torture and summary executions will be held to account.[7]

The letter was signed by seven of the most influential human rights organizations globally, all with sharp legal acumen.

Protests rang out, first from human rights advocates around the world, then from international organizations and agencies and civil societies formed to promote the world court, and then from those who had lived through the horrors of Lubanga's offensives, for they knew all that Lubanga had done, and they also knew the charges, as they stood, covered only a fraction of the suffering he had caused. The investigators had been the hope for these victims that more evidence would come to light to reckon with the crimes and the loss they had known. There was anger and suspicion that the Office of the Prosecution was not working hard enough or smart enough to gather the evidence. And as the pretrial continued through July and August and into September, and with the confirmation hearings still pending, the euphoric promise of a serious Court to end the impunity of warlords like Lubanga, so palpable a few months before, seemed to fade.

chapter 6

The End before the Beginning

Thirteen days remained before the opening of the trial. For a brief while it seemed all might be in order and a veneer of calm hung over the Chamber. There had been some changes in personnel. Judge Jorda would not preside over the trial proper; this would be the British Lord Judge Adrian Fulford, who had a reputation as a meticulous sovereign in a trial chamber. Lubanga's defence counsel had resigned in chagrin after the pretrial's decision and was replaced by the indomitable French defence counsellor, Catherine Mabille. Things started off equably enough with a provisional agreement about the schedule of witnesses. But there the short-lived honeymoon came to an end. Maître Mabille, the defence counsellor, complained loudly that the prosecution held evidence it was not disclosing. It was not clear at the time exactly what there was in these non-disclosed pieces of evidence the prosecution had gotten from the United Nations, and apparently it was nothing earth-shaking, but Maître Mabille did not seem to care much about what was there. She single-mindedly pushed the prosecution on the issue.

The Office of the Prosecution tried to explain that they had made summaries of the documentary evidence without mentioning names, including extensive summaries, which showed the gist of the material. But Maître Mabille wanted them anyway. She wanted to see for herself if there was some exculpatory material hidden away that perhaps the prosecution was keeping from her. And she drove her claim into the Chamber with a vengeance. She proclaimed the trial to be grossly unfair and worse, that the prosecution had these documents from the United Nations on the prejudicial condition that the information would be kept confidential.

The distinguished scholars who had convened in Rome in 1998 to finalize the Court's charter wanted to steer the Court clear of the raucous spectacles often seen in common law courts by making room for something more learned, more collaborative. Their idea, inscribed in the statute's Article 54, 1(a), was to soften the contest between the defence and prosecution and make room for something that built common ground between them. It was a stroke of idealism and perhaps even naive to suggest the Office of the Prosecution would work for both sides, assuming that the prosecution would step aside from the competitive fray of conventional common law courts and search for evidence in support of both sides.[1] The Court would be a hybrid of sorts, a nice idea, and Article 54, 1(a) settled into the Rome Statute with a warm glow.

But in the lead up to the trial, the warm glow went cold. Even before things got underway, courtroom conferences in the Chamber turned into jousting matches among legal luminaries, the sharptoothed Maître Mabille for the defence and the flamboyant prosecutor Luis Moreno-Ocampo. Then there was the very particular Judge Fulford abetting the two of them, gracious one minute and peevish the next. There would be media, and where there were media and the high stakes that came with media coverage, there were bound to be lawyers preening.

Even if the actors had been willing to soften their differences, the circumstances of Lubanga's case pitted the courtroom adversaries hard against one another. Though the charges had been limited, Lubanga's crimes were crimes of war, a lot of them fuelled by hatred between fierce enemies. And whether they wished it or not, the actors in the Chamber would line up just as the enemies had lined up in Ituri in 2002–3. For some, Lubanga was a hero, for others an arch-villain, and there was not much in between. The idea that the prosecutor could serve both sides was a good one in principle; but it was nigh impossible in practice since as far as any Hema knew or cared, the prosecution had come to convict their leader and place him in detention. The prosecution in Ituri would have to choose: be safe and side with the Hema, gathering support and exonerating testimony, or accept the risk of proving his guilt, living and working under the protection of armed guard.

And not only for the prosecution with its investigators. All who were in Ituri working in whatever way with the Court would have to watch their back. Court offices in Bunia would have to be secured with guards and iron gates. Court officials would need to be careful about making public the names of those who, even years before, had drafted reports linking Lubanga to atrocities or to recruiting children or to military manoeuvres, for these too would be seen as aggressors, and there were xenophobic archivists among the Hema who kept track of just who were friends of Lubanga and who were not.

The drafters knew it would be difficult to gather evidence of wrong-doing from a war zone and maybe they thought – or hoped – it would be easier if the Court's prosecutor put staff to work on documenting both guilt and innocence. There was a chance it would keep the investigators above the fray. The drafters were idealists, certainly, but they were not naive and they knew something about war. They knew that if the prosecution was going to carry this off – investigating incriminating and exonerating evidence both – it would need special allowances, and that is why the statute allowed the prosecution to agree with informers to keep what they gave them confidential.[2] This would protect informers from the risk of exposure: NGOs, international organizations, and anyone else with real information.

The prosecution made use of the provision when the United Nations agreed to hand over documents written by staff members who had worked in Ituri during Lubanga's rise to power, on condition that they be kept confidential. UN staff were within their rights, and so was the prosecutor. There were the reports from child protection officers and particularly sensitive ones, eyewitness accounts about child soldiers serving under Ituri militias. Somehow a bold child rights officer had even counted the number of child soldiers in Lubanga's army and listed the number of children and the names of their commanders. Reports from human rights officers and political affairs officers provided undeniable evidence of

Lubanga's crimes and all handed over to the prosecution with the understanding that the reports would not be disclosed. It was this that provoked Maître Mabille, who was always ready to discredit the trial for being unfair. She demanded that the prosecution disclose all evidence, knowing the prosecution was bound and unable. She claimed the prosecution had made the agreement deliberately to hide evidence from the defence.

On the morning of 10 June 2008, the trial participants assembled for a final conference on the matter, and things were tense from the beginning. The start of the trial was a few days away. The counsel for the prosecution was a respected war crimes litigator from Germany, Ekkehard Withopf, who had recently joined the prosecution's team. And after the customary welcome and niceties, Judge Fulford jumped quickly to the matter, boring in on Mr Withopf: "We'd be interested to know what the prosecution's suggestion is in relation to the appropriateness or otherwise of commencing the trial on 23 June when none of this material has been shown either to Mr Lubanga or the judges of this court."

Mr Withopf was conciliatory: "The Office of the Prosecutor is of the view the trial can nevertheless start on 23 June as currently scheduled by the Honourable Bench. The defence has been provided with alternative evidence. They cover the same categories of potentially exculpatory evidence. And on this matter, your Honours, also the Honourable Bench should trust the Office of the Prosecutor. I am saying this Mr President, your Honours, because the language of the statute specifically requires the prosecution to reveal 'materials that in the belief of the prosecutor are of potentially exculpatory evidence.'"

No sooner had Mr Withopf concluded his mollifying remarks than the judge pronounced himself firmly on the issue, as if he had been preparing his words in advance, as if it were a foregone conclusion and was ready to jump. "The judge," he said, referring to himself, "and the judge alone is the one to make this decision, not the prosecutor or the United Nations. The judge, and the judge alone has the obligation to ensure that any exculpatory evidence or potentially exculpatory evidence is fully disclosed."

"How otherwise," he continued, "could the Office of the Prosecution be allowed to make summaries of the material that will be provided to the defendant without the judges at any stage seeing the material or making any kind of judicial decision as to whether or not the approach taken by the Office of the Prosecutor is right?"

He paused to let the weight of his pronouncement settle within the Chamber. "Now that is a point that you need to address today."

The floor fell by default once again to Counsellor Withopf, who fished for a way to soften the judge's intransigence.

"The Trial Chamber will get to read the summaries, so indeed the Office of the Prosecutor has very deliberately taken the approach that the judge should play this very role."

"And how," replied the judge, "do we determine whether the summaries are adequate or are fair or are correctly directed, if we have not seen the underlying material on which those summaries are based? We will have to trust completely the quasi-judicial decision that will have been taken by the Office of the Prosecutor. Now how do you get round that problem, Mr Withopf?"

"Trust," he replied. A hush fell over the Chamber with the pronouncement of the word.

"There must be an aspect of trust in the Office of the Prosecutor, Mr President, and I hasten to add up to this point, there has been no evidence, not the slightest evidence that the Office of the Prosecutor is hiding potentially exculpatory materials."

The appeal to trust did not merit a reply from the judge, who flatly ignored Counsellor Withopf. Why, he asked, did the United Nations allow the prosecutor to manage the evidence contained in their reports and not the judge himself?

"Was the judge not the one to decide what was and was not admissible? And who, after all, did the UN think it was with its judgment about what was and was not to be made available?" He condemned the United Nations. He scolded Mr Withopf, saving his sharpest barbs for the prosecutor himself. The prosecutor was his favourite target. This brought the discussion with Mr Withopf to a close. Their discussion, he declared, had shed little light on the situation, and turning to the representative from the defence, Mr Biju-Duval, he asked if there was something he wished to add.

Mr Biju-Duval was emboldened by the judge's dismissive air towards the prosecution. He rose like a firebrand approaching a pulpit and with barely a word of introduction, set to shredding the prosecution. Accusations came fast and furious. Was the prosecution actively working on behalf of injustice? It seemed so. The prosecution's confidential agreement with the United Nations was a travesty, he said. He charged that it was eating up whatever justice was left after the prosecution's utter and deliberate neglect of juridical matters.

"It was," he said in a show of agitation, "a terrible, unbelievable situation."

"Why," he beseeched the Chamber, "do the United Nations and the prosecution both wish to deprive the accused of the means for a fair trial? Why is the prosecution allowing the confidentiality agreement to obscure the truth? There can be no truth. This now is impossible." He paused, as if he was about to throw his hands up in the air at the iniquity of it all.

"This is the first time the defence is saying this, what I am about to say, and we say it with the gravity it deserves, nor is this what the defence wants. The defence wants justice to be done. We have reached an impasse as we confront this scandalous situation that is not the fault of the defence team but rather that of the prosecution, hoarding evidence, if I may say it in this way, leaving the only solution remaining for the Chamber to decide the trial cannot go ahead."

Cannot go ahead. The words punctured the polite veneer of the Chamber. In their turbulent wake, the judge adjourned the session.

The Chamber reconvened a day later.

"Good afternoon," intoned the judge. He informed the Chamber this was to be a continuation of the status conference from yesterday, albeit brief, since the debate as far as he was concerned was over. "We have," he said, "reached a decision as regards all of the issues that were discussed. Some of them involve significant complicated matters, and in our judgment it would be inappropriate to set out our reasoning and our detailed conclusion in an *ex tempore* decision."

His decision would have to be written.

"We need only announce today one critical consequence of our decision, namely that the trial date of 23 June is to be vacated."

When the final decision was handed down two days later on 13 June, it was a facsimile of the defence's outburst dressed in legal clothing, proclaiming the prosecution's failure to meet the judge's conditions for a fair trial. The judge declared a stay of the proceedings. This brought the trial to an abrupt halt just as the defence counsellor had boldly proposed, even though at the time no one imagined it would happen. According to the judge, the prosecution had failed to renegotiate its agreement on keeping the UN documents confidential, however inconsequential these approximately 200 pieces of evidence were. They were, as Mr Withopf had tried to explain, of only minimal value to the defence since there was little there – he had seen them – that could be construed as truly exculpatory, and if anything, most of them would lead to an even more resounding conviction. But that mattered little. The trial was over. Lubanga was free to go, barring an appeal, and if he so desired, he was free to return to Ituri and resume his political ambitions.

Preparations to begin the trial on 23 June came to a halt. On that day the prosecution filed a motion to appeal the judge's decision. Thomas Lubanga returned to his place of detention to wait for the appeal to run its course. The long process of the appeal got underway at its laborious pace buried under briefs that soon filled rows of binders with legalese. Weeks and months passed. The pretrial had gone on far longer than anyone had anticipated, with the manoeuvring leading up to the trial over the order of witnesses and how they would be protected. And now the access to documents had buried the trial under a contentiousness so fierce that the trial in its third year had not even begun, and months would pass before it would try again.

For anyone who cared to read the repetitive discourse of the appeal there were no surprises. Pages went by and nothing of any relevance to the case of Thomas Lubanga was said. Ituri never entered the discussion for this was not about the DR Congo or Bunia or the people in the surrounding villages whose farms were despoiled and whose children were massacred during an eighteen-month siege by the man whom the Chamber had just recently declared free to go. The innocence or guilt of Thomas Lubanga was not in question, nor was whether the UN was in its rights to contract with the prosecutor to retain control over its documents. By all appearances the appeal was to decide which argument fit best with the appeals judges' reading of the statute: the judge's decision that gave a narrow reading of Article 54 or the prosecution's argument for a broader one. What was ultimately at issue was the judge's prerogatives, his entitlement, and his right to preside unchallenged in the Chamber.

It was now January 2009. Seven months had passed since the judge had stayed the proceedings on 13 June that ended the trial followed by the prosecution entering an appeal sending the matter to the Appeals Chamber. The Appeals Chamber made two decisions. The first was to agree with the judge that as long as any part of the evidence obtained by the prosecution from the United Nations was kept from the defence, it was difficult to have a fair trial, and it made no difference to the Appeals Chamber that the prosecution had made an agreement with the United Nations, because the prosecution should have tried to renegotiate the agreement. The Appeals Chamber obviously did not like Article 54, 3(e) in the statute that allowed such agreements and insisted on limiting the article only to special cases. When all was said and done, the decision of the Appeals Chamber stood behind the judge's contention that he, and he alone, was the final arbiter in deciding what kind of evidence was admissible in this trial.

The second made it clear that, even if the Appeals Chamber agreed mainly with the judge, he had gone too far. The Appeals Chamber did not like the idea of stopping the trial. The judge had flexed his muscle too flamboyantly. While the Appeals Chamber was in the throes of its deliberations, the prosecution was negotiating with the United Nations to disclose the documents, and since things in the Chamber seemed to be on the mend, the Appeals Chamber reversed this part of the judge's decision and ordered the trial to continue. Lubanga would not go free.

It was a minor victory for Maître Mabille, for it was her claim that the trial was unfair that had brought the Chamber to its knees and nearly liberated her client before the trial had begun. She saw now the worth of taking on the prosecution at every turn, making óbjections increasingly strident, for it was clear the judge had little patience with the prosecution, and he had a powerful compulsion to support the rights of the accused, no matter what the crime had been, even if this meant setting him free.

She had discovered that in this theatre of law she could carry on as she wished and needn't be bound by considerations of truth. She could disregard any suggestion that her client was well-known for his killings and rapes and recruitment of children. She could claim, as she would on many occasions, that he shone with the beneficence of an altar boy, one of the few politicians of integrity to come upon the Congolese scene, a defender of children's rights worthy of recognition. She now knew that no one in the Chamber would challenge her depiction of Lubanga as good and honourable as long as the judge was determined to show his commitment to standing so firmly behind the rights of the accused. The judge would open the door to letting impostor evidence rise to prominence. The prosecution could challenge this, of course, and have a say, but it would not be easy. These were crimes of war, and investigating them was not only difficult, it was risky; there was always room to undermine the prosecution's evidence, to find inconsistencies. The evidence would be bloodied, torn, and so disfigured that almost any claims about what happened could be put forward.

Meanwhile, Lubanga played the part of a bona fide politician, the leader of his people. He took impression management seriously. One day he was enrobed like a chief. The next, like a banker. Some days, he looked the part of an intellectual. There was nothing shabby about him, and the prosecution, if they wanted anyone to believe what he had done, would have to show another side of this Lubanga and reckon with Maître Mabille's glowing portraits, and with a judge so ill-disposed to the prosecutor that any cogent argument about Lubanga's crimes would have to run a gauntlet of motions that did more to protect the accused than attend to the victims.

The United Nations, strangely enough, ended up on the Chamber's blacklist. It never did get a decent hearing and was repeatedly censured as the bad boy of the proceedings. This was all the more surprising as United Nations staff members had seen more than anyone what Lubanga had done. They knew better than anyone what had transpired and had eyewitnesses. They had counted the dead and rescued the children. They had tried to negotiate with Lubanga himself and fallen prey to his deceptions. The United Nations had shielded the population in Ituri from the chaotic rampages of Lubanga as best they could and, once they had an adequate contingent of peacekeepers, fought to protect people from his atrocities. Staff members had risked their lives to stop him from criminalizing politics in Ituri, stealing land, decimating villages, and eviscerating his neighbours. Now the Chamber was asking the United Nations to give Lubanga's defenders access to privileged information.

The appeal did nothing to diminish the malaise of the trial. The Chamber wars carried on as before when the trial resumed in the New Year, falling as ever to quarrelling, as if this were the only modus operandi. Here they were, on 12 January 2009, and they were arguing as before about how to protect those who took the risk of serving as witnesses in the trial. It had earlier been a question of protecting the UN and its staff members and their contacts in Ituri, and now it was the witnesses themselves, some of whom had been victims. They now would have their faces projected on every Internet screen that cared to display them. They would be branded public enemies in parts of Ituri. On this day the prosecution rose to announce in the Chamber that after much consultation protective measures would be put in place: voices would be distorted, pictures of the witnesses projected for public on a screen would be altered, and pseudonyms would be used.

The defence rose in objection.

From the perspective of the defence, the trial was hostage to an over-weaning humanitarian impulse, and this was not fair.[3] The defence claimed it was the right of the public at large to know the case, and it was the obligation of the Chamber to bring the case before them. A majority of the witnesses had requested full protection, and this meant they could not be identified outside of the courtroom. As far as the defence was concerned, this made the trial

a kangaroo affair where a few men and women – presumably bi-
ased – would decide the outcome of the proceedings. It was
Mr Biju-Duval again. He wanted the witnesses, even those whose
families could be identified and harmed, to be exposed, for how
else could their client, Mr Lubanga, be sure the way he was treated
was open to proper scrutiny?

chapter 7

The First Witness

On the morning of 28 January 2009 the trial proper was scheduled to begin.

The first witness from Ituri, once a child soldier, had been sequestered in his room for days while the Chamber debated procedures. He was ushered to a room adjoining the Chamber and told to wait until called.

Fatou Bensouda, the assistant prosecutor, was at her most regal. The public gallery that looked down on the Chamber was filled with visitors. The guards had their instructions. The media were there. Dignitaries were there. The Court officer announced, "All rise," and the three judges, the one chief judge and two associates, entered in their robes while the defence team huddled round their newly appointed chief counsel, Maître Mabille. All appeared ready.

But it was not quite. After an exchange of niceties, Judge Fulford brought forward a new procedural wrinkle, one that seemed oddly timed with the witness fresh from the DR Congo waiting in an adjoining room. Rome Statute Rule 74 directs the Chamber to forewarn a witness – *instruct* is the preferred term – what might happen should the testimony reveal the witness had committed a crime: the witness could be prosecuted. The prosecution looked around. The defence shrugged. Could this really be an issue? It all seemed grossly improbable, since the first witness, at least, had been a child soldier under Lubanga and was well under the age of fifteen at the time, a minor in other words, and not eligible for prosecution either under Dutch or Congolese law. The judge seemed nevertheless quite possessed by the matter.

It was his considered opinion that witnesses should be cautioned about revealing crimes they might have committed, since there was the possibility of incriminating themselves and, yes, the witness should be told, it was clear. The judge gave his august thoughts on how it should be conveyed and who, for example, would be qualified, since certainly it would have to be a seasoned lawyer with bona fides. Many of the witnesses were bound to have been soldiers at the time – that was their job to engage in war with all its consequences – but was this now the right moment to warn them their testimony could be held against them?

"Mr Walleyn ..." said Judge Fulford.

Mr Walleyn was a thoughtful human rights lawyer representing a group of victims participating in the trial, and the witness waiting in the wings was one of them. The judge wanted to know whether he had advised the young man that he should be careful about saying something that could incriminate him.

"I did give information on a number of concerns, but I do not think it was exhaustive in giving information on the rule you have just mentioned."

"Then, Mr Walleyn, in our view this needs to be done, as it were, coolly and quietly and in an unhurried way. These concepts are difficult enough for lawyers and judges, but for civilians who have no familiarity with court proceedings, they require some explanation and some time to understand them."

Mr Walleyn gathered his papers.

The judge turned to Fatou Bensouda and suggested she too, as the spokesperson for the prosecution, have a visit with the young man, once Mr Walleyn was done.

But there was no time. Mr Walleyn would have just enough time to speak with the witness as he made his way to the Chamber. Meanwhile the judge continued to concern himself with procedural issues, the protection formalities, raising and lowering the blinds. "Oh yes," he said. "And Mr Walleyn, please, if as a result of your discussions with the witness you are confident that he is ready to proceed and the warnings have been given, we will then proceed to 'the commencement of the witness' evidence."

"You will let us know, won't you? You will send a message so we can resolve these issues in advance of the witness being brought into the court."

"Certainly."

The judge could be furtive in moments like this, with so much to consider. The defence sought to submit an application about the quality of the translation. He would consider that later.

Yes, no, he said, "What we are determined to avoid is the witness being brought down just outside the door to give evidence and for there then to be a hiatus that prevents him from coming in. Nothing can be more guaranteed to destabilize a witness who may be feeling nervous."

They waited. The defence complained about documents missing from those they expected from the prosecution. It was a familiar refrain. A pause. A brief recess was declared and the Chamber momentarily adjourned and reconvened in an hour.

"All rise."

"Be seated. Court is in session."

"All well, Mr Walleyn?" asked the judge.

"I was able to address the request of the court."

"Good."

The judge motioned for the blinds to come down.

Only a select few in the courtroom could see the young man enter – the Chamber had agreed to give him the pseudonym Dieumerci – as he looked around and finally was directed to a small table with a microphone facing the judge. This put the defendant Thomas Lubanga immediately to his left. Lubanga took his measure of the young man who was about to give evidence against him.

The Court usher approached the witness with a piece of paper: "I solemnly declare that I will speak the truth, the whole truth, and nothing but the truth." Three times the sound equipment failed and three times the witness repeated the oath.

The witness appeared composed. He told the Chamber why he never finished the fifth grade. On his way home from school in the small town of Fataki a band of soldiers stopped him with his friends. They were dressed in camouflage fatigues. He knew their uniforms because they were Lubanga's men from the UPC, Union des Patriotes du Congo, and had guns. He knew they were fighting against the Lendu and he remembered the soldiers telling him, "The country is in trouble and young people must mobilize to save the country." He was eleven years old at the time and scared.

Fatou Bensouda asked him, "Among those school people who were taken away, were you one of them? To the training camp?"

"Yes, yes I was one of those who were taken to the camps."

"And when were you taken to these camps?"

Dieumerci seemed not to understand, as if his mind were elsewhere.

"I want you to recall how you were taken to the military camp and if you can remember, when you were taken as you have said."

"I cannot remember. I was very young and so I cannot remember the date but I know very well what happened. It happened while we were walking home from school."

"And who were you with? Now be careful ... the names of those who you were with when coming from school ..."

"I only had my friends with me."

"How many?"

Once again the judge raised a flag of caution. The witness might be identified by his friends, so at his signal the blinds that would hide him from view dropped down, and enhanced protective measures were put in place while the young man gave over the names, the ones he could remember.

Ms Bensouda continued, "You said you were going with your friends and you were taken, and you've given us the names of your friends. Who was it that took you? Who came to take you with your friends while you were going home from school on that day to the training camp?"

"UPC soldiers."

"What kind of weapons did they have?"

"Rifles, SMGs [sub-machine guns]."

"And how many of them came to take you?"

With each query, the witness appeared to hesitate more. Something was bothering him.

"I can't remember how many, but I know they came with their chief who was with them."

"When they came to get you, did they tell you anything?"

"Yes."

"What."

"Our people were in trouble and young people must mobilize to save our people."

"And did you respond?"

"Yes."

"What did you say?"

"That we were too small, there were others who were older."

"What did you mean?"

He was about to answer when the defence objected to the prosecution asking what the young man meant. There was a pause. The judge overruled the objection and turned back to Fatou Bensouda. And in that moment, that pause, the young man began to waver. He was unsteady when Fatou Bensouda returned to ask him what he wished to say about being so small while others were bigger.

"Well, there were children among us. We were children, and how could it be we were put in with older people?"

"And did you go with the UPC soldiers on the day you say they came to you? Did you go?"

No answer. His face was impassive. Whatever had come over Dieumerci had now fully possessed him.

"I gave an oath in court that I would say the truth, the whole truth and nothing but the truth, and I find myself in a delicate position."

Fatou Bensouda asked him again if he went with the soldiers, and again he stopped short of answering.

"What do you mean 'delicate position'?" asked Fatou Bensouda.

"I gave an oath to speak the truth."

"We only want you to speak the truth."

"The questioning is giving me problems," he said. His discomfort was palpable. He seemed to lose focus as he looked around behind him.

The judge broke through the silence. "We may be in the territory of Rule 74," suggesting the witness was now worried about incriminating himself. Had he not warned the Court the witness should be properly advised?

A scent of dread was unmistakably in the air, though not because of Rule 74. It might have been his capture as a young boy, the beatings he had received in Lubanga's army and the sound of guns, the deaths he witnessed, the trauma of a sensitive boy faced with the horrors of war. And there to magnify his anxiety was the man who had taken his youth sitting twenty-five feet to his left, a man who just might one day seize him again. Better, he seemed to say to himself, to stop there.

The blinds came down and Dieumerci was led gingerly out of the room. A ten-minute recess was called. The judge had deputized Mr Walleyn to speak to him once again. If it was Rule 74, Mr Walleyn was to put the matter to rest. If not, then perhaps he could, with tact, give reassurances.

Nearly an hour passed before the Chamber reconvened.

The judge dispensed with his customary niceties and turned straightaway to Mr Walleyn.

"Are we likely to encounter further problems?"

"I can confirm, Mr President, that the witness is now ready to testify. And if I took some time, it was because I wanted that all guarantees could be obtained that the integrity of the evidence is granted."

"We are very grateful to you."

"Thank you, Mr President."

The blinds were lowered as the witness re-entered, flanked by guards.

"Good afternoon," said Ms Bensouda.

Dieumerci said nothing.

She took up where they left off. "You were telling us about the UPC soldiers coming to take you and your friends. You were going home from school when that happened."

"No," he said, "that's not the case."

"What is the case then? Can you tell the Court?"

"What I said earlier was not what I intended to say. I would like to say what actually happened myself, not say what some other person intended for me to say."

"We are only interested in what happened to you and the truth."

"It was in Ituri, that is the truth. I was in primary school. And at the time there was an NGO helping children. And my friends and I went there, and they took our addresses and told us they could help us. So the NGO took our addresses and we went home again."

Dieumerci's appeal to the truth was his only polite option now for escaping the rush of memories and threats surrounding him in the courtroom.

"Thank you. But before this, did you go to any training camp?"

"I will tell you." He paused.

"I am not asking you about what the NGO told you or what they said to tell us."

It was too late. The young man was in rapid retreat.

"I am asking you now whether you attended a training camp."

"No," answered Dieumerci.

Fatou Bensouda turned to the side, exasperated. She looked up at the judge. "Mr President, just a moment … if I may ask for ten minutes' break, if that is possible, and I am asking this because obviously I think what happened earlier on has had some form of impact on the witness. I may be wrong, but I think, Mr President, either we can have a break or maybe we go into closed session to explain some information that may need other parties to validate."

The courtroom was in disarray. An hour before the trial's main actors might have thought the witness's hesitation was a momentary aberration that could be settled with some assurances; but assurances had been to no avail. The recess only hardened his resolve. He would not speak about joining Lubanga's UPC army, or about the forced march into Camp Bule, or about the training, or the battles he fought or any of the events that had earlier convinced the prosecution Dieumerci was their choice witness and the best to take the stand first thing.

The judge, the prosecution, and the defence offered each their own conjecture of what had occurred. The judge wondered whether there might be some kind of threat against the witness, which was unlikely, as his living quarters were virtually quarantined. It would be difficult for anyone to get past the guards. It was Fatou Bensouda's theory that the witness was worried about something or someone who might know who he was, who would pass on the word and threaten his family or what was left of them and those who had helped him demobilize. More protective measures were needed, and she would discuss this with the Victims and Witnesses Unit. Just to steady the poor fellow.

Meanwhile Maître Mabille counselled the Chamber to take the young fellow at his word: was it not clear the boy had been lying from the moment he took the stand? He had never been a child soldier. Whoever arranged for him to come to the Court had coached him and perhaps even promised some money.

As the witness left the room there lingered in the Chamber an odd aroma, not a smell so much as a hint of something singularly unpleasant. It was the residue fear leaves when it is exposed, not a fright but the discomfort of fear that comes from something prolonged, a persistent presence and a reminder that something terrible had happened.

～

Dieumerci had in truth been seized by Lubanga's men, along with many other children, when the fighting began in September 2002. He endured the gritty training regimen to become a soldier and was on the front lines by the time he was twelve. He was a shy boy, more fit for school than the battlefield, and his father, who happened to work for Lubanga as a bodyguard, took it upon himself to salvage the boy and bring him home. Dieumerci went back to school, but after all that had happened he was no longer able to do his work. He had trouble concentrating. Fate was not kind to him. He was seized as a deserter and taken back into Lubanga's forces. Once again, he was rescued and returned to his father's house. His mother had disappeared, and there was another woman in the house. Relations with his father became worse. He found his way to a demobilization centre for child soldiers, and there he stayed. He would be protected. He learned a trade.

The man in charge of the demobilization centre was a good man. He saw in Dieumerci a traumatized child, and he told him about the investigators who had come from The Netherlands and about the trial against Lubanga looking for someone to testify and said to him maybe it would be good if he agreed. Maybe it would help bring his ordeal in Ituri to a close and give him a new start to his life. His choice. Dieumerci had always been a thoughtful boy and he thought it over: any life was better than this one. The man at the demobilization centre warned him the courtroom would be a battlefield of its own.

When six years later he had reached the stand in Chamber One in the looming white building, it was winter in The Hague and he knew nothing about winter. There was no one to care for him as there had been in Bunia. He was cold and alone, and there it was, the fear. It was all tolerable at first. He answered some questions. They explained some of the rules and he thought he understood. When he walked into the courtroom, there was Lubanga himself looking at him, and he realized no amount of preparation could have made him ready for that moment. The lady asking questions wanted to know if he had become a soldier for Lubanga, and he knew if he said yes it meant he had done something bad, and maybe there would be consequences; it would turn the Court against Lubanga, and there could be consequences. It was confusing. He did what he had learned to do, hide in a ditch, make himself small, run when he could and seek refuge wherever he could find it. The only thing open to young Dieumerci as far as he could see was to deny all that had happened, to hide from the terrible things in his young life.

Later that day, Dieumerci retired to his quarters. The judge called the Victims and Witnesses Unit to ask if more protection would help. And since there were few alternatives, it was agreed new measures would be considered. There was the weekend. Food was prepared three times a day. Five days later the Victims and Witnesses Unit recommended there be more protective measures. A curtain would be installed between the witness and the defendant that would make eye contact impossible. Dieumerci would not have to worry about Lubanga's eyes boring into his back. The trial carried on. Dieumerci's father gave testimony for three days, an outspoken man difficult to trust, and then another weekend and two more days while Dieumerci remained indoors away from the cold as days passed. On Wednesday, 11 February, thirteen days since Dieumerci's ignominious departure from Chamber One, the car came once again to bring him back to the stand.

chapter 8

A Child Soldier in the Chamber Wars

"Would the witness take the stand?"

Dieumerci made his way through the middle of the courtroom between the defence and the prosecution towards the small table at the centre of the room opposite the judges.

"Good morning," said Judge Fulford.

"Good morning," replied Dieumerci in French.

"How are you feeling?"

"I'm feeling fine."

Judge Fulford gazed down at him from the dais. The judge was meticulous in both his appearance and his preparations; it was partly this that allowed him to rule his demesne with a rarefied air of benevolent command. He was courteous to a fault. Should a minor error of diction or fact occur in his Chamber, he would hasten to correct it with grace, knowing there would follow an equally gracious expression of gratitude. He was ready to extend a noble hand, and he expected deference in return.

To the judge's far right was Thomas Lubanga Dyilo, still as a stone in impeccable banker's attire, and in front of Lubanga was his defence team, though it is probably more accurate to speak of Maître Mabille's team, since it is difficult to think of Maître Mabille belonging to any team other than her own; it made more sense to think of Lubanga playing on hers. On either side of Mabille were her loyal aides-de-camp, Mr Desallier and Mr Biju-Duval. Opposite the defence, on the other side of the room, was a symmetrical array of tables and robed counsellors for the prosecution. Behind these sat the lawyers for the victims.

Dieumerci had to pass between Maître Mabille on his right and the prosecution on his left to seat himself in the centre facing the judge.

With a quizzical look the judge asked, "Are you going to be all right to give evidence today?"

"Yes."

"Jolly good."

The judge briefed the Chamber on the arrangements to make Dieumerci more comfortable. A curtain would be drawn between where Dieumerci sat at the place for witnesses and Lubanga's line of sight, so he would never have to feel Lubanga's gaze. And if ever he had to speak about his friends or family, there would be paper and pencil available to write down their names instead of having to say them out loud.

Dieumerci listened attentively.

"Our witness number 298 will continue to be known by the name of Dieumerci. This is a pseudonym that does not have any capacity to reveal the true identity of this witness."

Clear enough.

"Now, Dieumerci, a few days ago when you were with us, you were asked a number of questions about things that happened to you in relation to your schooling, some friends of yours, and the UPC. Would you like at the beginning of today to have the opportunity simply to tell the story in your own words? Would you prefer to do it that way to begin with?"

"Yes."

"Good. Take your time and do it in your way. Tell those of us sitting in court what happened to you. In your own way."

There would be no interrogation.

"I am going to tell you the truth," he began.

"I was in primary school at the Fataki Mission, fifth year. Everything was going well until the war between the Lendu and

Gegere [Hema] broke out. Other people became involved in that war, and from that time onwards there were problems in school.

"One day when I was coming back from school with my friends. We were walking through the market and we met up with UPC soldiers, lots of them, and there were only six of us – myself and five others. And they said to us, 'You children, we're going to take you for training so you can become soldiers and do your part for the security of our country.'

"I told them I was a schoolboy – it was difficult for me and the others because we were children."

When he first appeared on the witness stand, Dieumerci had been afraid to tell Fatou Bensouda that he had gone with them and all he had gone through. Not this time. He said he tried not to go with them, but there was no choice. He told her his group walked and walked for two hours to Bule camp. And when they got there they were put into groups with names like Company B and Company C. At the camp, he said, they were pushed into shacks with nothing except what they were wearing. He remembered only that most of them were little children who knew nothing of war. When they arrived, they were confused. The commanders barked orders at them. They made them run and jump and, when that was too difficult, they taught them songs.

Mainly they beat them. They beat them from the moment they arrived. If anybody talked, he was beaten. If he did not answer them, he was beaten. He was beaten when he did what they told him. He was beaten when he did not. He was beaten when he found clothes that fit him and he was beaten when he had clothes that hung off him. He was beaten when his gruel was good and filled him up and beaten when his gruel was watery and left him with an empty stomach. The beatings turned a young man into a mean little animal. This is what they wanted. So when the boys took their positions just like the older boys showed them, along the side of the road, and extorted money from drivers or whoever passed by, taking whatever those in the car could pay, the boys asked for more and pulled them from the car and beat them till they gave more. Beatings were given and received and given again. Young men who had never been beaten, who had grown up in a village among mothers and aunts and uncles in the bosom of a family, became ferocious little animals.

Once Dieumerci began to speak in the chamber, he blurted out how one day led into the next, how the veteran soldiers took them into the forest to cut a piece of wood for practice rifles they would carry around like real guns. They were just sticks of wood, but if anyone lost his, he was beaten, and if anyone screamed, he was beaten even harder.

"Whenever somebody tried to flee, they were beaten or killed," he said. "I saw people being shot at for trying to escape. I saw it with my own eyes.

"The training went on using pieces of wood as firearms until a plane landed in a nearby airstrip carved out of the forests bringing uniforms and guns. And from then on, planes landed every day, sometimes three times a day." As far as he knew, they came from different places, carrying "clothes and equipment, plastic boots, rubber boots. The training went on because there was going to be a war, and we had to be shown how to go to war. We were taught. Things were written on a big board in front of us so we could see how things were going to happen. None of us knew anything about war, but we listened and tried to remember and then they took us to a field where we practised going to war.

"The uniforms were just thrown out of the boxes here and there. We were small and most of the uniforms were big and we wore them anyway. There were big boys and some of them got small uniforms. It didn't matter. Sometimes you were given small boots for big feet or big boots for small feet and it didn't matter because you had to run in them anyway."

Once some men in uniform came and said anyone who felt sick should go to one side and they would call a doctor. But there was no doctor, they just beat them. They beat them for no reason. And they beat them even harder if there was a reason. When the real weapons came, they had to guard their weapon with their life because anyone losing their weapon could be beaten to death.

"A few days later the cartridges came and each had thirty bullets in them. 'Keep the cartridges,' we were told. If you fell asleep and someone took your cartridges, you had to go in front of everyone, where they would beat you harder than ever. They taught us to shoot. We crawled along the ground with our guns, and they put us in different positions, and then we had to shoot at a target. If you were not in the right position you could be killed, because some of the boys were taking hemp and they were not in their right minds and they could hit someone. They put a target up, a red and white paper, and we aimed for the white colour inside the red circle. And really it was difficult for anyone who never did it before, loading and reloading, while they are shouting and you are going as fast as you can. You pressed on the button and off it went, and if you didn't hit the target after one or two tries, the trained soldiers beat you.

"After that, some of us guarded the camp at night, but mainly the younger ones were the bodyguards of the commanders who liked to have young children around them for their bodyguards. They liked them with guns, even though most of us had just learned to shoot, but we would shoot anyway, and they took us, and if we had to shoot, that is what we did. They liked that. We were supposed to guard their houses or around the perimeter, and if the commander did not like us, he would beat us, or others in his house would beat us. We were told that was the UPC way, to beat and pillage, and if you did not do that you were beaten. Or killed. That is why so many took drugs, and with drugs they would do anything, like they would set up roadblocks and take money from anyone they could."

Dieumerci did not like the hemp and he did not drink much, but everyone else did. And he apologized to the Chamber because he could not remember everything. The booze and the hemp and the beatings had all melded together in his memory. There came a time when his group moved from Fataki to another camp not far away, and later some of them were moved to Largu, a few days' walk where things were worse, because around Largu in the small town of Bule his group was ordered to attack the Lendu. He was afraid. They were told what they had to do, but once the boys had smoked the hemp everything went crazy, and his group was running here and there. Dieumerci remembered only that he was alive from one day to the next. They must have killed quite a few people, because he remembered young bodies strewn across the battlefields and his group going through them chopping off heads and sticking fingers in the sockets to gouge out the eyes. He remembered that one day he went with the others into town, and there on the dirt track that ran between the shops of Largu was his father. He hardly recognized him. His father seized him by the arm and took him into a small local place to eat. He said he was going to take him home to Bunia and put him back in school. Dieumerci knew what could happen to him if he was caught running away like a deserter, and his father knew it too.

He returned to school in Bunia, this time a secondary school. He was not sure when, but after a while there was a school holiday, and he went with his uncle in his car to visit relatives in the town of Centrale in the direction of Fataki. On the way the car was stopped by boy soldiers at a blockade, just as he himself had done to others when he was a soldier with guns pointing in the faces of the people inside. They were forced out of the car and threatened if they did not give more ... and more. The boys took everything. Suddenly one of them looked hard at Dieumerci and recognized him from the Bule camp, and they seized him because there was a reward for capturing a deserter. The boys beat him on the way back to the camp. They beat him so severely he would never recover from the wounds of the sticks landing on his back and arms and legs. His breath would never come easily again. They threw him in a small hole that had been dug in the ground for prisoners and kept him there for two days. Then they let him out and gave him a filthy uniform.

He was a soldier again. A shipment of arms was coming from a place nearby, and everyone ran to the airstrip in the forest. After that Dieumerci followed the others to the main UPC camp at Centrale. He did not remember how long he stayed there, but it was not long before he saw in the camp a man who looked like his father.

"It was my uncle," Dieumerci smiled, appearing fatigued. "He came into the camp and spoke to the commanders. It was OK with them. We went as far as Nizi where my father was and I met him. We spoke to each other and we had something to eat and then we got into another vehicle and returned to Bunia."

Dieumerci was unhappy at his father's house. As far as he knew, his real mother had died and another woman had taken her place. He was afraid to venture out for fear of being spotted by a UPC soldier and seized again as a deserter. He left the house only to make his way quietly to school and waited till dark to return home. One evening he heard an announcement over the radio for boys like him who had escaped from armed groups about a demobilization centre where child soldiers could go for help if they brought in a weapon. Dieumerci was received by a kindly man who worked for an NGO and learned there was money from abroad to house the boys and girls at the centre if there were good reason. He moved in.

When Dieumerci finished, he looked around the Chamber.

"Dieumerci," the judge said, "you've done very well. I wish I could speak as well as you."

He was composed, a contrast to his last appearance. This time it was the defence who were agitated. The judge warned them off. He would not have them "picking away at the edges" of the young man's testimony. But Maître Mabille was implacable. She was convinced that Dieumerci's simple and straightforward narrative was in fact a carefully constructed lie, and she was equally convinced it was the mother of Dieumerci who, conspicuously absent up until then, would tell them the truth of what happened. Where was she, Maître Mabille wanted to know. They were pretty sure that Dieumerci and his father were doing their best to keep her hidden from view.

It was Mr Desallier who stepped forward for the cross-examination. He had some questions about how Dieumerci had come to be a witness, who had suggested it to him and why. He wanted to know about his schooling, mainly about which grade he was in when he claimed to have been taken into the training camp. Dieumerci had earlier said it was the fifth grade, but Desallier had seen school records that seemed to show he had gone through the whole fifth grade. Was Dieumerci telling the truth here? Hadn't he left the school when he was taken to Camp Bule?

"My question," said Mr Desallier, "is when exactly were you recruited? Is it true that you told the Office of the Prosecution that you were in the fifth form in primary school at the time you were recruited?"

"Yes," said Dieumerci.

"So what is the right answer, fifth or sixth?"

"Fifth."

"So you say you were unable to complete the fifth grade because you were abducted prior to Christmas that year? Is that it?"

"That's correct."

But Desallier did not believe it. Dieumerci had said sixth grade at one point and now he said fifth. If it was the fifth year, what about the school records that showed he might have completed the year. Was he lying about being abducted? Dieumerci became confused. As far as he could remember, he had never finished the fifth, or if he had, he had finished before Christmas. Mr Desallier pressed on. What about the commanders in the army camps where he said he had been? Did he really know the names of the commanders, or had he made them up? The defence was sure he was covering up the truth. What did Dieumerci have to say about that? The father, for example. Dieumerci claimed to get along poorly with his father, but the defence believed Dieumerci and his father had in fact teamed up to deceive the Court. Mr Desalier held up a form submitted by Dieumerci to apply for victim status and argued it was the father who had been with him throughout the application process. They were in cahoots from the beginning.

Had not his father put him up to all this? The defence argued the father had been with his son every step of the way. Had they not done well for themselves? They had gotten out of Ituri and into The Hague. And after The Hague they would go somewhere under witness protection, the boy would go to school, and finally the father would have some modest means, quite the improvement over standing guard outside Thomas Lubanga's residence. The defence never said as much but implied they were here for personal gain. Had they not cobbled together a story of abductions and beatings and misfortunes in the camps and covered their dubious tracks as best they could?

And why was the mother nowhere to be found? Dieumerci said she was dead, that she had died some years ago. It made him sad to think about it because he had then to put up with another woman in his father's household he did not like. The father said yes, Dieumerci's mother had been forced to flee, and as far as he knew – it was a time of war, after all – she had been killed in the melee of events. Dieumerci was disturbed by the matter and preferred not to talk about her.

The defence insisted the two of them knew where she was and were keeping her away from the Court because she knew the evidence they were giving was false. They said she knew about the elaborate conspiracy the father and the son had concocted, and the two of them were doing everything they could to keep the mother away from the proceedings.

Maître Mabille's defence team had pressed Dieumerci's father about the mother. The father's answer did not satisfy them and now, with Dieumerci on the stand, they asked again. Was she really dead? How did he know? If she was not dead, where was she?

Fatou Bensouda asked for the floor. She was concerned the defence would press Dieumerci on the matter of whether his mother was alive or dead, and if they were not satisfied, they push him on the issue of where she was. It was guaranteed to traumatize.

"We just want to make an application, under Article 68, for the Chamber to protect the psychological well-being of the witness." She hoped that would do to keep the defence from asking whether the mother might be alive or not and just exactly where she was. She appealed to the judge that if there had to be questioning, could it be limited to asking about when she had died? Nothing more.

The defence refused. They suspected the father and the boy knew she was alive, and they wanted to confront the boy to see what he would say.

Maître Mabille's right-hand counsel stood up, Mr Biju-Duval.

"I insist on the fact that this is not a gratuitous question. There are three very simple points to be borne in mind. The defence has serious reasons to believe that the witness was not enlisted as a child soldier under the circumstances as described and that there is some falsehood here. Second point: The defence has serious reasons to believe that concealing the existence of his mother corroborates the first lie. So the defence thinks that the fact that his mother being alive was concealed and the existence of the second wife who took care of this child was also hidden as a way of obstructing in-depth investigations in order to protect the initial lies concerning the reality of enlistment as a child soldier. This question is therefore at the heart of the defence's theory. It is not an unwarranted question seeking gratuitously to discredit the witness. So I wish to make it known to the Bench that this question is crucial, because it enables us to determine the veracity and sincerity of the two statements given. And that is what I would like to bring to the attention of the Bench when it rules on the matter."

The judge retired to his chambers.

He returned after a short recess, quite unconvinced by Fatou Bensouda's appeal for mercy. Certainly one should be gentle with the boy. "However," he said, "we are persuaded that given the attack that is made on the credibility of this witness and his father that this area is one that the defence is entitled legitimately to explore."

Shortly thereafter Mr Desallier asked the witness if he knew when his mother died. Dieumerci simply did not know.

"When you heard about your mother's death, did you talk about your mother with your father?"

"Of course we talked about it."

"Do you remember the last time you spoke with your father about your mother?"

"I can't remember it."

"Do you believe that there is a possibility your mother is still alive?"

"No, that never crossed my mind. Any other time I might be able to give you an answer. Right now I have problems that are upsetting me."

chapter 9

The Paladin, the Warrior, and His Lordship

On 29 May 2009, the Court heard moving testimony from a member of Lubanga's inner circle who had decided, as a matter of conscience, to give evidence against his former leader. He described what had happened to the children they recruited, how they were treated, and how he had come to visit one young boy who had been captured by the enemy and placed in prison. The boy would not give up his gun that he had come to believe was his surrogate parent. It was a vivid rendering of the impact of the war on children. The judge interrupted with his usual apologies to advise the prosecution counsellor that her questions were imprecise and missed the point. She should be more attentive to the age of the children involved. After all, how did she know these children were under age? The counsellor was not pleased with this interruption but, with no other choice, she asked the witness to estimate the child's age.

The witness could not be sure. The judge intervened again, displeased that she had not properly guided the witness in making the age precise. Her examination was now in the lurch, but she obeyed. At that point, Maître Mabille rose with her own complaint: how accurate could the witness be after all? Her objection was sustained by the judge, who urged the counsellor to do better. She rephrased the question. Maître Mabille then raised another objection that now the counsellor was repeating herself. Sustained again. The two of them, Judge Fulford and Maître Mabille, had successfully blockaded her questions until her orchestrated interrogation was fully scrambled.

The fractious interaction among the main actors pulled the trial down into a morass of tactical ploys and objections. Maître Mabille, the courtroom warrior, took to the match eagerly. The prosecutor was more than ready, seasoned trial lawyer that he was. The judge might have mediated or stayed on the sidelines, but instead he stirred the pot by handling the prosecutor with impatience and Maître Mabille with kid gloves, abetting their belligerence. Maître Mabille threw out challenge after challenge upon the proceedings, knowing the judge would more often than not take her side and knowing also it would drive a wedge even deeper between the judge and the prosecutor. It was hard not to pity the prosecution's counsellors, who bore the brunt of the judge's pointed interventions. He would challenge them. He would tell them they had not phrased their questions properly or sustain an objection from the defence that seemed trivial. On contentious matters of procedure, the judge frequently ruled against them. The trial was becoming a war of attrition among three legal rivals: the prosecutor, the defence counsellor and the judge.

The prosecutor, Luis Moreno-Ocampo, was accustomed to a good rumble. He was a crusader. He was in the case to win it, but more than that, he was a lawman with a mission. He wanted to come to the aid of the people of Northeast Congo and elsewhere, where warlords ran roughshod over vulnerable people and their livelihoods. In a documentary film[1] he can be seen sporting a white suit alighting from a helicopter onto a grassy stretch in front of a rough-hewn school somewhere in the outer reaches of Ituri, marching at the head of a bevy of handlers past crowds of children, speaking as he strides across the terrain about the Court and about peace in the DR Congo.

He is quite serious about his mission. He is also fond of the spotlight, and this has brought him his share of detractors. But for all his critics, Luis Moreno-Ocampo has the credentials. He was the public prosecutor in Argentina who dared take on the "Trial of the Juntas," the first trial since Nuremburg that brought high-ranking military commanders into the dock and charged them with mass murder. These were ranking generals from the Falklands War, three former heads of state and notorious officials who had wallowed in corruption and terror, disappearing dissidents in Argentina for years. No one dared challenge them in court except Luis Moreno-Ocampo. His colleagues warned him. His grandfather, who was a notorious general himself in the Argentinian army, warned him. His mother said he was risking his life. He ignored them. Between 1984 and 1992 he prosecuted nine senior commanders and sent five of them to jail in the most famous trials in Argentina's history, and then he moved on to track down more corrupt officials.

When he arrived in The Hague he was no longer the biblical David taking on the Goliaths because here, as the first prosecutor in a new world court, he was himself a Goliath among other Goliaths. He had become the first man of global justice in a place where the terrain was very different from Argentina. He knew how to navigate the legal badlands of his home country, but in The Hague he was subject to the tinkering of diplomats and the manoeuvrings of international organizations. It was as much politics as justice that concerned them, and the protection of their sovereign legal prerogatives. The prosecutor would have to mind his political fences.

But that was not his style. Making enemies came with the territory. From the beginning, Moreno-Ocampo was convinced that the Court, if it was to make life better for the victims of murderous regimes, would have to go after heads of state, prime ministers, and senior ministers, for they were the ones to be stopped if human rights were to have a chance. He modelled himself after the celebrated Italian prosecutor Giovanni Falcone, a legend for his pursuit of crime lords in the course of the Maxi trial against the Sicilian Mafia in 1987 that charged 474 Mafiosi and convicted 360 of them, 119 in absentia. Falcone's was a heroic mission and one that earned him the Italian Medaglia d'Oro al Valore Civile from the Italian government and some years later the distinction from *Time* magazine in 2006 of being among the real heroes of the previous half century. Falcone also had his share of enemies. The bomb that reduced him and his car five years later to shrapnel was so powerful it rivalled earthquakes on the Richter scale.

Moreno-Ocampo was forever pushing the limits of what the ICC was willing to do. He wanted the Court to flex its muscle and arrest high-profile offenders. Lubanga was a moderately small fish. In subsequent years, he would go after Omar al-Bashir, the president of the Sudan; Uhuru Muigai Kenyatta, one of Kenya's most senior politicians; the son and deputy of Mohammar Khadafi; and the ex-president of Côte D'Ivoire, Laurent Gbagbo. Here was Falcone rounding up the Mafiosi. He had as many critics as allies, and not only from African leaders who circled their wagons to protect their own but from conservative commentators and international diplomats and academics who disapproved of his style. He should have known the conservative inclination of international officials and members of the international legal community to preserve the status quo by containing controversial figures. He should also have known his style would set him on a collision course with Judge Adrian Fulford.

Both Fulford and Moreno-Ocampo had had distinguished careers and wore their accomplishments conspicuously. Both had large public personae. Moreno-Ocampo was a passionate man. Judge Fulford was dispassionate. The substance of the case and the suffering caused by the crimes were paramount for the prosecutor, while the judge was, first and foremost, a jurist. It was orderly procedure and courtroom convention that mattered most. When they met in the courtroom, they abetted each other: the more colour the prosecutor displayed in his interventions, the more the judge stepped in to keep things black-and-white. On good days they barely abided each other; on others, they did not.

As the trial stumbled to an end and as the prosecutor himself neared the end of his term of office, complaints against him intensified, some of them reasonable and some of them not. He was as self-serving as any high-profile lawyer. He loved the perquisites of power. His efforts to arrest Sudan's Omar al-Bashir were hasty, and he did it knowing there was the risk that al-Bashir might become more murderous than before. There were complaints that he overreached his remit. There were complaints that he tended more to his legacy than to the particulars of his cases.

I met him on a number of occasions. He was ready to talk, perhaps because he felt he could use this minor exposure to project a strong image that would somehow protect him from his emboldened critics. But it was also because he was an open person by nature. He was easy to like. He could turn a room of strangers into allies. I asked him on a few occasions to speak about what was happening in the Lubanga trial. He hesitated at first because he thought better of speaking about specifics and moved on, as he was wont to do, to the larger issues of the trial. The intermediaries concerned him, those intrepid souls in Ituri who helped his office gather the information they needed. There were the disclosure wars. Protection for the witnesses – should he have gone as far as he did to protect them? It simply wasn't fair, he argued, to expose them when they had done as much as they could for the children and the Court. And deterrence. Why were the warmongers heading for cover where the Court was investigating? There's something you can write about.

He was not a man to compromise. He stood tall for justice and was impatient with the posturing of the self-proclaimed big shots who occupied the upper reaches of the legal establishment. This, as much as anything, made him particularly contemptuous of Judge Fulford, whose posturing was singularly rarefied and who took his reign of supreme authority seriously in his Chamber. Moreno-Ocampo was just as wilful as the judge, and it made the two of them a combustible combination. In time the escalation of their wills would hold the trial hostage. For those who knew Moreno-Ocampo, it was no surprise how little fazed he was by the wagging finger of the judge, for he was accustomed to pushing the law and its procedural props aside where there was justice to be done.

Maître Catherine Mabille was a very different story. She relished a courtroom duel as much as the prosecutor, but she was not the crusader he was. It was the chess match of the trial that counted as far as she was concerned. She honed her arguments to dissect the argument of others. Her talent was to expose the weaknesses in the arguments of her adversary; this was her forte, the tactical push and pull of the courtroom. She had found her métier in war trials, defending those who had been accused of heinous crimes, finding holes in the accusations against them.

She had defended Paul Bisengimana, one of the worst of the war criminals from Rwanda and the mayor of the infamous town of Gikoro, where a thousand victims took refuge in a church and where he pressed his townspeople to slaughter them all. Which they did. Maître Mabille's work was to distance her client from the events, make his involvement seem less than it was and, in doing so, diminish the horror.

Maître Mabille was known for her defence of war criminals, urging courts to give the benefit of the doubt to the worst of defendants who had given nothing of the sort to their victims. Her clients included mass murders. And yet, somewhat anomalously, she fancied herself a human rights advocate. She was president of France's chapter of Avocats sans frontières. I found this curious until I asked a prominent human rights lawyer how it was possible and he smiled as he explained that the Avocats sans frontières chapter in France was not like the others. It had veered away from the majority of chapters. In France, Avocats sans frontières does indeed champion the defence of human rights, except here it is the rights of the accused and less so those of the victims.

Her passion was for legal combat. I was not surprised, as we exchanged emails in the lead up to my visit with her in her office in Paris, that she fished for the angle I was taking: was I for or against Lubanga? That was important if I were to qualify as a visitor. She finally relented, though it seemed only reluctantly. She saw no reason to waste time with someone who was unlikely to contribute to her campaign in the courtroom.

Her office was in a gentrified quartier of Paris in an older remodelled building. The salon d'attente was well-appointed, old armchairs arrayed in a symmetrical gravitas on Oriental rugs, a contrast to the welcoming waiting area outside the cluttered working chamber of Luc Walleyn, the kindly representative for a group of victims. Her office assistants busied over me until I accepted coffee with condiments. After a wait and considerable commotion, someone came in to announce that Le Maître was ready.

"Finalement, bienvenue," she said, "asseyez-vous." Before I had settled in the straightback chair, she immediately asked. "Le jugement ... êtes-vous d'accord?" By the time of our interview, the conviction and the sentence had been handed down and she was now preparing the appeal.

"That was my question to you," I replied.

"Certainement pas," she insisted.

So much for introductions. She sat with her back to a bay window in a spacious office dominated by a large wooden desk in an imposing chair, where she presides and where there is no pretence of making her visitors feel equal. She sits unabashedly across the abyss of her escritoire, leaving others to sit in straight-backed wooden chairs.

I asked her how she was selected to lead the defence team and about her successful defence of Paul Bisengimana, the butcher of Gikoro. She was not interested in speaking about any of that. It was my position on Lubanga that interested her, and when she realized I did not object to his conviction her argument against the conviction shifted into high gear.

"The trial is *pourri*, rotten to the core," she said. "It is the materiality of the case, the assemblage of facts themselves or the lack of them. They would have never led to a conviction except this was the Court's first case. You must agree."

"An open question."

"But that is the only question. And there is only one explanation. Lubanga would never have been found guilty had this not been the first case at the Court. After all, to acquit the man would have weakened the Court. I know that. It is a travesty. To lose the case was unthinkable for the Court."

"You mean, just because it was an important case ..."

"No, not just an important case. It was *too* important. And the prosecutor could prove nothing. He was unable to prove the soldiers were under fifteen – never – and he did nothing to prove Lubanga was himself responsible, never. That was his job and he did not do it. Lubanga himself issued a decree asking his hierarchy to release from duty any child under fifteen. That was Thomas Lubanga's own decree, you understand. The charges against him are erroneous. *Erroné*"

"But Maître ..."

"*Écoutez* … I have done my research. Have you done yours? Did the prosecutor do his? My team and I spent seven months in Ituri. We examined every one of the witnesses claiming to be child soldiers, and we found where they went to school. We copied the records. That's right, we copied the records and sent back twenty-five kilos of records. And what did we do with them? We examined them, and we found all but one of the witnesses claiming to be child soldiers had been registered at school when the Prosecution claims they were soldiering."

I nodded.

"They were in school, not in Lubanga's army. They were never soldiers, because they were in school, and we have the records to prove it. You see, that's the way with Lubanga's Hema: they educate their children. They send their children to school, not to fight, and if you know anything about Lubanga himself, you know he has a university degree. There's no child soldiers from the Hema in Ituri. This is what I'm telling you."

"What about the video of children carrying guns in uniform as Lubanga's guards?"

"Please, do not speak to me about this video. It was a farce. There was a young boy with a gun, and what does that prove? Was he a soldier? Was he brought to the trial? Of course not, because he was not a soldier. And the others, all of them and not a single one telling the truth. They all lied."

"Some were persuaded to lie and some were paid," she declared, placing her pen with care on the desk's glass top. "They all lied."

"Pourri. Le cas est pourri, complètement pourri de haut en bas." The case is rotten, top to bottom.

Maître Mabille carried on with assurances that Thomas Lubanga was far from the butcher of Ituri and was instead its benign leader seeking peace among brothers and sisters in the region. She had masterfully defended her client. This was admirable. But she had also orchestrated a case that would not just give Lubanga a fair hearing but would defeat her adversary. She was in the courtroom to win, and to do that she had boldly and self-assuredly made questionable assertions, some of them unjustifiable, as far as I could see. The Chamber was incapable of stemming this tide of seemingly untenable allegations.

The judge did little to contain her. He was genteel to a fault and a master at deflecting contentious matters with pleasantries; he was indeed the perfect English lord. And yet underneath that veneer was a commanding air, an uncompromising knife-edged belief that he was the giver and author of the law, who would direct the trial as the conductor of an orchestra with the flick of a baton. It was with this authoritarian hand that he resolutely held the prosecution at bay and gave Maître Mabille free rein to feed the fires of dissension.

Maître Mabille had read these courtroom dynamics as any astute lawyer would, taking full measure of the judge's contempt for the prosecutor and doing what she could to exploit the tension. She reminded the Court of the prosecutor's failure to meet his disclosure obligations, whether they were really all that serious or not; she complained about delays and insistently so; she hinted the prosecution was paying off witnesses even if this was highly unlikely; she complained about the excess of witness protection measures that, as far as she was concerned, was the fault of the prosecution, and she did so counting on the judge's penchant for holding the prosecutor to account. At first the discord in the Chamber had been nothing more than alarming, but as the contest escalated, a relatively simple matter could bring the trial close to a premature end.

This made for a stormy Chamber. It also made it difficult to have a reliable picture of the case. The adversarial method in the common law tradition assumes truth is best served when two sides put forward competing versions of events. But this works only when the actors are dispassionate enough to play with restraint and more or less by the rules, because when things become excessively adversarial, defeating an opponent becomes more important than the accuracy of the evidence.

I very much wanted to speak with Judge Fulford, as I had with the Prosecutor Luis Moreno-Ocampo and Maître Mabille, and especially about the tension in his Chamber. He has spoken very little in the wake of the trial, and perhaps that speaks for itself. He has his apologists, though even they could hardly deny that his Chamber came off the rails in many regards. I tried repeatedly to arrange a meeting, to little avail, and regrettably so, since it is important to know what brought the trial so often to the brink of coming apart. He is one of the few who has said nothing on the matter. He has written only briefly of his concern that, in spite of attempts, he was unable to persuade the Court to hold at least a portion of the trial in the Congo. And, like others, he lamented the unusual duration of the case. But that is all. I would have liked to ask him why he so fervently disdained the prosecutor and his staff, even when it threatened to add to the animus in the Chamber, since, for the most part, the counsellors for the prosecution were conscientious to a fault. His disdain for the prosecutor coloured much of the trial and could not help but intensify the turbulence in the courtroom.

The trial became a victim of its own importance. The spotlight was on, and into the spotlight stepped legal divas, each with a prominent performance record in international or criminal law. Perhaps it seemed fitting to bring in illustrious figures for so momentous a trial. But there were consequences: it was the case of the rapacious Thomas Lubanga that should have been in the spotlight and should have been bigger than any of them. Instead, the importance of each – the paladin, the warrior, and his lordship – loomed larger than the importance of the case itself. The efforts of each to prevail and show a redoubtable presence in the courtroom overshadowed Thomas Lubanga's own criminal schemes to prevail in Ituri. And, like King Pyrrhus, any one of them would have gladly won the battle of the trial even if, as a consequence, it meant sending the case to the rubbish bin.

chapter 10

Witness from the Front Lines

Christine Peduto has spent most of her life in war zones working to save children from disasters. She was in Bosnia during the worst of the Serbian onslaught in 1992. She was in Afghanistan before that. She was in Iraq with Handicap International, in charge of caring for children with limbs lost to landmines. In the late 1990s, Save the Children asked her to manage their program in the Democratic Republic of the Congo, working first from Nairobi and the regional office, then later from Kinshasa at the national office, followed by a move to Kisangani. Not long after, the United Nations peacekeeping mission in the Congo asked if she would help them in Bunia, the heart of Ituri. It was 2002 and the violence was spiralling out of control.

Most young people do emergency service in war zones for a short time and move on, as they become war weary and want to return to normal life. Some find a slot in one of the lumbering donor bureaucracies. Some work in the headquarters of human rights organizations. Some sell insurance. Not Christine Peduto. She is among those who stay on the ground saving kids, crisis after crisis, and not because of her penchant for travel or attraction to different cultures, but because she is a front-liner. Front-liners live in camps or in shipping containers or in the back rooms of small hotels. The job is not pretty. Front-liners may drink in the evenings. They may have transient lovers. They may regale each other with stories late in the night, and some are reckless, but they are always who they say they are, and they are always ready at six in the morning with the truck running and their kits or computers or bandages or whatever they need in the course of the day.

Christine Peduto is not one to take pride in what she did in Ituri, though it was considerable, for she was the first child protection officer to arrive in Ituri at the height of the conflict with the job of caring for children. There were kids adrift in the streets without parents, some abandoned, some starving, and some taking refuge in transit centres after escaping from armed groups. She had gotten the peacekeepers onside to protect these kids. She had coordinated the contributions of NGOs and UN agencies who had come to help once they knew that someone like her was on the ground. She worked closely with the peacekeepers when they travelled to areas in turmoil to ensure they knew what to do for families and children in trouble. She met with commanders to inform them of their international obligations. She wrote the reports that went before the Security Council detailing the numbers, ages, and militias of the child soldiers, and these reports in turn shaped the humanitarian response of the United Nations. She was never that interested in bringing attention to her role in all this. And that is why she was uneasy on 15 November 2006 when she appeared as an expert witness for the prosecution at the pretrial in the lead up to the trial proper.

"So you are Madame Peduto," said Judge Claude Jorda as she entered the pretrial chamber. She would testify on more than one occasion in the Lubanga case, and this was the first. "For now, I would like you to stand. You won't have to stand for the whole of your hearing, but I would like you to have your swearing-in standing up."

A piece of paper was passed to her. "Could you please read it? Thank you very much." The judge continued: "Madame Peduto, I would like to ask you now that you are here before the Court. Do you feel at ease?" She nodded.

"You are going to have to answer the questions that the prosecution will ask. The prosecution wanted to hear you in the context of the Lubanga case, and the judges will also possibly ask you questions, but normally the cross-examination takes place later. So you will be available until then."

She remained silent.

"Please identify yourself, your date and place of birth.'

"I am Christine Peduto. I was born in 1968 in Marseille in France and I am French."

The questioning came around to her role in the Congo. "And can you please expand the information you are providing to the pre-trial chamber in respect of you having been in Ituri – the time you spent in Ituri."

"My first move to Ituri was at the beginning of September 2002, and then I participated in another mission in the middle of September 2002. After that I was present in Ituri permanently beginning in February 2003 with my MONUC [Mission of the United Nations in the Democratic Republic of the Congo] contract."

"For how long, Ms Peduto?"

"Until the end of June 2004, officially."

"And where did you have your offices?"

"Bunia."

"In the context of the mission in September 2002, to your recollection, did the name Thomas Lubanga or Thomas Lubanga Dyilo come up?"

"Yes. Obviously the question of the large number of children who were members of armed groups in Ituri was central to the work of our section, and in addition there were other problems that affected children that we dealt with. The name of Thomas Lubanga was mentioned in the conversation and briefings given to us by our military observer colleagues."

"And in these briefings, Ms Peduto, what information on Thomas Lubanga Dyilo was provided?"

"Mr Lubanga was described as the leader of the Union des patriotes Congolais, the leader of the group who were in charge of Bunia. This was what I received from my colleagues in the briefing on the security situation, on the composition of armed groups that were present all over the territory, with details as to the high presence of children in these military groups, including the one of which Mr Thomas Lubanga Dyilo was in charge."

Her responses were terse. She noted simply her meetings with commanders and functionaries and children, the NGOs who tried to help them and how they were funded. Where they met. The records they kept.

The first day's interrogation went late into the afternoon. Towards the end of the day, Mr Withopf of the prosecution placed his papers on his desk and paused. "Did there come a time, Ms Peduto, when you had the chance to meet Mr Thomas Lubanga Dyilo?"

"Yes, I did have the opportunity to meet Mr Thomas Lubanga at the end of May 2003 in the company of MONUC colleagues."

"Can you please inform the pretrial chamber what the purpose of the meeting was at the end May of 2003 with Thomas Lubanga Dyilo?"

"It took place at the end of the day, if I remember correctly, on 30 May 2003. It had been requested by the head of the MONUC office at the time, Mr Alpha Sow. And he was in the company of another UN official, Mr Gomis, who was in charge of policy affairs in the Kinshasa office. He wanted to speak specifically with Mr Thomas Lubanga about the arrival of the multinational force[1] in Ituri in addition to other issues, such as massive human rights violations that we were witnessing and the child soldiers who were in the ranks of the UPC."

"And can you please let us know where the meeting took place?"

"In one of the residences of Mr Thomas Lubanga, north of the town. I think that would have been in the Mudzipela neighbourhood. I think it is."

"Who was present at the meeting?"

"Apart from Mr Alpha Sow, the head of the office of Ituri, and Mr Gomis of MONUC Kinshasa, I was there, the head of security in Ituri for MONUC, Mr Thomas Lubanga Dyilo himself, and other UPC members whose names I don't remember."

"And was there a particular reason, Ms Peduto, as to why you took part in that meeting?"

"To talk in detail about the use and recruitment of child soldiers by the UPC militia."

"And do you recall, Ms Peduto, whether Thomas Lubanga's residence in the Mudzipela district of the city was guarded?"

"It was guarded, and I remember especially because this is something that shocked us. It was guarded by children, armed children, not only armed children but they were wearing uniforms. They were guarding the residence; that was obvious in the way they approached the vehicles of MONUC we parked in the compound of that residence and the way they accompanied our entry into the residence of Mr Lubanga."

"And do you still, Ms Peduto, have a recollection about the age of these children?"

"They were young enough for all of us to be shocked during our visit. I remember seeing one who was particularly small, but at the same time, it was nearly nightfall, so we did not carry out a detailed investigation on the membership of the guard. I remember seeing a young child who was less than fifteen years of age. I didn't really take note of the others."

"You mentioned that these children, including the one child you were sure was under fifteen years, that these children were armed. What sort of arms did they have?"

"I think they had Kalashnikovs."

"And how did you feel at the time when you went to Thomas Lubanga Dyilo with the purpose to talk about the use of children in the UPC militia and you arrived at his residence and you saw children, including young children, guarding his residence?"

"We thought it was somewhat provocative, as the MONUC officer was present at the meeting, and especially since it was at Mr Lubanga's request that the meeting was held at his residence and not the MONUC offices. I felt it was a provocation of some sort by Mr Lubanga."

"Did you actually manage to talk to Mr Lubanga?"

"Yes, towards the end of the interview, because it is true that much of the interview was focused on the arrival of the multinational force and the UPC's position on withdrawing their troops, the way of organizing Bunia without arms. It was being discussed at the time. So a great deal of the interview focused on the arrival of the multinational force. At the end of the meeting we mentioned the matter of the number of children who were members of armed groups and the responsibility of Mr Lubanga. I explained to him what MONUC was supposed to do in regard to these children and the fact that we were recording the actions of the commanders

– not only myself, but all the military officers. I also talked about the various resolutions and reports that had been drafted within the United Nations. I talked of protective measures that had been planned by protection agencies in order to facilitate the reintegration of these children into their families. I also remember suggesting at the end of the meeting, which was getting a little long, an interview with somebody of his choosing to discuss the modalities of helping these children and the way in which MONUC and the protection agencies could offer to help these children get back to their families. This was a proposal within the framework of a working meeting with the UPC."

"And from what I understand, based on what you told us, you had a chance to address these matters related to the recruitment and use of children within the UPC armed group with Thomas Lubanga Dyilo. Was there any reaction on his side?"

"No, no. I mentioned that the DRC had ratified the Rome Statute, because that was something important for us and something we wanted to raise awareness about amongst the armed groups. As regards prevention of recruitment and re-recruitment, no, there was no reaction. Later, after that meeting, the various commanders of the UPC who were members of the cooperation committee that had been set up in the wake of the Ituri Pacification Commission never wanted to have a working session either with the MONUC protection section or with other UN bodies. These requests for working sessions were always declined – no follow-up was given, no."

Two-and-a-half years passed before Christine Peduto testified again in the Lubanga case, this time before the trial proper on 5 July 2009, with Judge Fulford presiding. The pretrial chamber under Judge Jorda had been collegial. This chamber was different. Legal manoeuvring seethed under the surface. She knew the prosecution would encourage her to steer clear of the many incidents of rape and torture that Christine Peduto knew had occurred, because the prosecution had long-since retreated into keeping the charges as they were. They were taking no chances in this confrontational atmosphere. The defence would scour her previous testimonies for material they could use to trap her in inconsistences, to prove she was never as sure as she appeared about what happened in Ituri. They would look for any part of her testimony, no matter how minor, to use as proof of her partiality or her lapse of attention or perhaps a zealousness that could have clouded her memory, even the smallest piece that would discredit the whole.

As the session began she was asked if there was anything particular she needed before taking the stand. Most witnesses wanted to hide their identity, and Christine Peduto could have disguised her voice had she wanted, but she cared little about her own protection. All she wanted was a sheet of paper with brief notes to keep before her with details of cases and numbers should they be needed, for she knew she would have to be accurate to a fault. It was hardly a request to raise suspicions but the defence objected. Positions were taken and rebutted. Legal bickering went one way and the other, the judge siding with the defence in what was becoming a predictable pattern. Finally Christine Peduto was informed by order of the chamber that no notes would be allowed during interrogation, leaving her to sit at her place empty-handed in the courtroom, aware the judge would do little to keep predators at bay.

The counsellor for the prosecution, Ms Solano, approached.

"Do you remember the youngest child soldiers who had passed through the demobilization process supported by the NGOs and the UN in Ituri during your years of service in Ituri?"

"Certainly."

He was an eleven-year-old boy taken from school when he was ten, who had served for a year before risking an escape to one of the transit centres in the town to register for demobilization. She knew all the details – where he was from, his commander, the location of his engagements, and more.

How, Ms Solano wondered, did she recall this in such detail?

Christine Peduto grimaced and shrugged her shoulders.

"In what context did you have access to this information?"

She had a disarming way of pursing her lips, pausing in conscientious reflection before speaking. She explained to the chamber step by step what happened when children who had been in one of the armies, whether Lubanga's or those of his enemies, arrived at a transit centre. They were taken first to the security officers at MONUC. If there were weapons, these were taken. The children then came to the child protection section, where she did her best to engage them. She preferred not to be in a hurry. She asked them questions, and if they did not answer at first, she waited. Who were they, who were their parents, where were they living now? How old were they, and did they have any birth records? How had they ended up in the armed group, and where were they trained, what was it like, whom did they serve under? She wrote it all down.

"So you kept notes as a way of documenting your meeting with children?" asked Ms Solano.

"Correct. For the database."

Eyebrows were raised among those who were hearing for the first time about so meticulous a body of evidence on child soldiers.

"Do you recall how many cases you recorded?"

"Six hundred and eighty-seven up to May 2004, and that includes all the cases that were registered."

"And how many of these were under aged fifteen."

"Two hundred and twenty. The number who had been affiliated with Lubanga's UPC was 167." She explained these numbers included only those she had interviewed. There were many others, many more from other groups, and more from the UPC who never fled the ranks. The children she met were only those who sought help in the transit centres.

Judge Fulford was on the verge of closing the session. He had started the day distraught that someone had disturbed some papers he had left on his desk overnight and he had lashed out at the custodians and the security people. Now, late in the day, he was tired. He apologized for his ill temper. He had meant no harm.

"Ms Solano," he said, "we are going to encounter what I've previously described as the Cinderella syndrome: in two or three minutes, the tape is going to run out and we're going to all turn into pumpkins. Would it be convenient for you to break off at this point, or are there matters that you wish by way of final detail to deal with now?"

"Your Honour, if I may just ask one or two final questions to close this topic for the day."

"Most certainly."

"Ms Peduto, for the 167 children that you've said have been associated with the UPC and who were under fifteen years old, are you able to recall or estimate what proportion of these had been recruited or used in the conflict by the UPC between roughly mid-2002 and mid-2003?"

It was a crucial question, for if there were more than a few, and if Christine Peduto were to be believed – as seemed probable – it would be hard to imagine any other outcome than a conviction and a lengthy sentence.

"A very large majority of the children I interviewed participated in armed conflict. Well, to give you details on these 167 children, I think I will have to consult my notes before I speak more precisely." With that, she pursed her lips and looked up at the judge.

"A point," Ms Solano said, "on which the witness might be allowed to check her notes overnight."

It was difficult not to be moved. She had the candour of a schoolgirl, simply attired and hesitant in her own unassuming way. She spoke sparingly in French, furrowing her brow as if she were making a particular effort to give a temperate account of what had happened, and if there was something she did not know or remember, she would say. There had been quite a few testimonies in the trial, victims and child soldiers, investigators and politicians, but few like this. Some of them had been elusive and vague. Some had outright lied out of fear. Some had embellished their testimony out of self-interest. As for Christine Peduto, she did not venture beyond what could be corroborated or vouchsafed with documentation or numbers.

During the next day's examination, in this same matter-of-fact way, she explained that, of the 167 kids who had escaped Lubanga's forces whom she interviewed at the transit centres, 71 were under the age of fifteen at the time they were recruited, and of these all had been involved directly or indirectly in armed conflict There was no reason to doubt the transit centre records. Some were girls, and there was not one of them in her records who had not been raped.

It was in this same quiet fashion that she recounted the rest of the story she had begun during the pretrial of her visit to Thomas Lubanga with MONUC officers to discuss disarmament and child soldiers. She was asked to provide more details. She explained she had carried legal documents with her, extracts from the Rome Statute showing articles that made recruiting child soldiers a punishable crime, along with descriptions of the crime.

And Thomas Lubanga's reaction? He was not terribly impressed, she said. He looked away without comment, as if he gave the matter little importance.

"What happened after that? Did he hand over his children? Did it seem to make any impression?"

Christine Peduto responded that she had in fact heard the UPC had given an announcement to Radio Okapi covering Ituri that had to do with demobilizing child soldiers. Someone had heard it or thought they had. When she tried to get a copy of the text, it was not possible. There was nothing at Radio Okapi, the UN-sponsored radio station. The UPC gave her nothing. Maybe it had been aired and withdrawn.

"Any evidence that the UPC contacted MONUC or other organizations to hand children over?"

"I never actually saw it and no one was able in the end to find it."

"Nothing more?"

"I know that some of the children who left the UPC went to a particular transit centre, and there were requests by MONUC and other child protection agencies to the UPC for assistance, but there was never any follow-up to our request for a meeting, that is an official meeting with the members of the UPC as regards that matter."

"Did recruitment of children by the UPC continue throughout the time that you were responsible for Ituri?" That question went to the heart of the matter.

"It did."

So much of the trial turned on the question whether Lubanga was fully aware that his armed groups were taking in children under the age of fifteen. Christine Peduto had addressed these questions as an eye-witness. Her testimony might well have been a turning point in the trial.

Instead, it was hardly mentioned again. The judge seemed to find nothing of Ms Peduto's testimony worth considering in his summation two years later. He gave greater weight to casting doubt on the veracity of some of the witnesses, wondering if any of the child soldiers could be believed, chastising the prosecutor and his team for their behaviour but never once mentioning the straightforward, fact-driven accounts of Ms Christine Peduto.

The charges seemed at first to be incontrovertible, even if they hardly did justice to the gravity of the crimes. But very little could be taken for granted; here was a world where obvious facts were churned into their opposite and fabrications were pressed into fact. Had the plodding pace not been so tedious, the chamber might have been laughable so curious were the claims and counterclaims, but it was deadly serious. There had been 13,500 child soldiers, perhaps more in Ituri during the years 2002 and 2003, many of them under Lubanga. Still, at the conclusion of the trial, Maître Mabille claimed that not one of those witnesses who had come forward as child soldiers could be considered credible.

chapter 11

Muting the Victims

Many of the child soldier witnesses who came to the stand in The Hague were, like the first witness Dieumerci, possessed by the fear of reprisals and the dread of standing before the man who would not have thought twice about taking their lives seven years before. Invariably, their testimonies were shaky and unpredictable. Once the examination started, they were easy prey for Maître Mabille and her team of relentless interrogators, who would circle a witness until a hint of an inconsistency surfaced, along with the suspicion that the young witness had been coaxed or coached, suggesting some motive for hedging the truth.

As one witness followed another, the brutalities in Ituri that brought the case to international attention and now to the International Criminal Court seemed to fade from view as if they were a matter of increasingly incidental interest. The less said the better about what actually happened as far as Maître Mabille was concerned. Judge Fulford seemed to agree. The other two judges went along, even if on occasion one of them did dutifully remind the Court the price girls had paid under Lubanga's command: the rapes, the enslavement, the inhuman treatment. By rights, the team of prosecutors should have stood firm for anything that showed the gamut of Lubanga's crimes, but they did not, preferring instead to do whatever it took to get a conviction, even if this meant neglecting some of the worst of the war crimes. This left almost no one to hold up the full measure of what Lubanga had done.

Except for the victims. And for a brief few months in the first year of the trial it looked like the victims might just bring a dose of real justice to the trial, just as the Court founders had hoped they would.

~

The conviction had grown in the years leading up to drafting the Rome Statute that victims would have to be in the courtroom. They were too important to leave out, and not just for the Court's individual judgments about one defendant or another but for the grander mission of calming tensions in the wake of massacres and mass crimes for places like Srebrenica in Bosnia or Gikoro in Rwanda, where there was little hope for reconciliation by simply declaring one or two persons guilty and sending them to prison. It was not enough for the victims to stand in the back of the room with no solace except the satisfaction of seeing the accused led away after long years of litigation. Retribution, the drafters decided, was not enough.

This was a bold step, and as the new Court got underway, its flagship feature of including victims was applauded by those who wanted a truly new Court that did something more than point the finger and send the perpetrators away. This added a different dimension to justice, a restorative dimension compensating the victims instead of only punishing the accused.[1] It was certain to be difficult. Hundreds of victims were sure to bring their grievances to the trials, all of them seeking at least to register the harm they had suffered. The Court would struggle with processing so many registrations. There would need to be reparations at some point, however incalculable the damages had been. No one pretended it would be easy, but when matters came to a vote among nations in 1998, there was hardly a member state that objected to the principle of bringing victims into the courtroom.

A large number of victims did come forward in the Lubanga trial, and all had to be interviewed in Ituri and screened. One hundred and thirty-nine victims were eventually invited to participate in the trial, and the Court appointed a counsellor to manage their affairs. There were three groups of them, each group with its own legal representative. And though the victims themselves did not attend the trial in person, their three legal representatives were there and diligently intervened to remind the Court of its obligations to the victims. It was a thankless job. The prime actors in the chamber might have been prepared to honour the statute in word but were far less ready to honour it in deed.

On 22 May 2009, only a few months after the trial began, one of the representatives retained by a group of twenty-seven victims stepped forward with a serious proposal. He reminded the Court that the charges, important as they were, had little to do with why most of the victims had come forward. On behalf of his clients he petitioned the Court to include in the charges brought against Lubanga the crimes of sexual slavery and inhuman or cruel treatment. The point was obvious: even if Lubanga were found guilty of the one original charge, very few would qualify for reparations. The victims' petition did not say whether this meant adding new charges or allowing the Court to include these crimes as aggravating elements of the existing charges. The wording was vague enough to allow either, but it made clear the trial served little purpose as far as they were concerned if it did nothing more than hand a light sentence to Lubanga for using children in war.

The victims were a conscientious group. They had filled out forms, taken part in interviews, and told their stories. Some had been taken by force into the camps, been shoved into makeshift lean-tos in the training centres, where they slept on top of other young recruits; some had been tortured; some had seen friends shot dead on the spot for disobedience. There were women among them who had been raped and kept in bondage and then sent away to be stigmatized by their home community. The Court had vetted them carefully and weeded out those looking for personal vendettas or a payout, keeping those who appeared to follow their convictions. They also had to be ready to risk their security by taking a public stand against Lubanga.

The judge was far from pleased. Even before the victims came forward when there were only rumours that something was afoot, the judge was resistant to the prospect. This was not something he welcomed. Involving such a number of victims would upset the schedule of events, witnesses, and hearings, and the case was already behind. A few days previously he had groused over the matter in the chamber. Had anyone heard? Were the victims in fact bringing a petition to the Court to modify the charges, and how could this be? The trial was getting behind, and modifying the charges at this stage would take time.

The victims' petition asked the chamber to "trigger a procedure for a modification of the legal characterisation of the facts." The Associate Judges Benito and Blattman both agreed with the petition, and since they were two out of the three judges, theirs was the majority decision for the chamber. They agreed there would have to be limitations on what new elements could be brought to the trial, but the trial was after all a process of discovery, and new information was bound to emerge. A dubious interpretation of the statute's regulations[2] was no reason to prohibit the consideration of new facts.

Judge Fulford took grave exception. Either the charges could be modified, he said, or they could not, and as far as he was concerned there was no middle ground, no room in the existing charges for giving greater emphasis here or there, since in his view the charges either stood as they were or they did not. He preferred the way they were. That was final. He did not put great store by the victims' reading of the statute's regulations used to justify their petition, since there were, after all, other provisions in the statute that, he argued, took precedence.

This was the view he took in his minority opinion. The affectations of law's language are presumed to guard against those who would tamper with its clarity. But strangely enough these affectations can make the language even more vulnerable to calculated abuse, since any assertion whatever, especially forceful ones in the language of the law, comes off with the ring of truth. The judge claimed that "once the trial has begun, the charges cannot be amended nor can additions or substitutions to the charges be introduced," as if this were the legal gospel. He built his case against the petition on a thick bed of references to Rome Statute provisions that claimed the petition was inconsistent with other important provisions in the statute. Soon there was a mountain of paperwork piling up against the petition, none of which actually considered whether the chamber was serious about accurately assessing the crimes Lubanga had committed.

This was to Maître Mabille's advantage, of course, and she went after the victims' petition with renewed vigour. One might have expected something different from the prosecutor, Luis Moreno-Ocampo, who was a reputed champion of the people and a crusader for justice, and yet here he too was standing against the petition joining the defence and the judge against the victims. He may have reasoned that a more direct involvement with the petition would have made his job that much more difficult, more claims to prove, more questions to answer, more time taken. I was not alone in wondering what this meant for global justice, seeing the judge, Maître Mabille, and the prosecutor more or less united in opposition against the victims who put forward the petition.

The three of them, each in turn, asked the Court leave to overturn the majority decision of the two associate judges and send the matter to the Appeals Chamber.

And there the matter stayed for months as the trial continued. The Lubanga trial in a nearby chamber carried on as before, leaving the Appeals Chamber to plod along with its deliberations in parallel. Witnesses came and went. The trial chamber heard evidence of the very atrocities the judge wanted barred from discussion. Child soldiers told the Court of being taken by force and put into camps, of their escape and finding their way to places where they would be cared for. Many witnesses claimed they had seen friends massacred. Had it not been for the social workers in the reintegration centres, they would have stayed in Lubanga's armed forces till they were injured or killed. A young girl came forward who had been repeatedly raped and become pregnant and bore a child by a man who later gave her to another man who raped her and made her pregnant again. The trial carried on.

Buried in appeal, the victims' petition faded into the background, almost as if it had never happened. The law could do this, pile motions and delays on top of an issue until it suffocated under the tedium of procedure. And time was a factor. The more the trial advanced, the more difficult it was for a new slant on the charges to take effect, no matter what the Appeals Chamber would say. The voice of the victims became fainter till it could hardly be heard. The judge, meanwhile, steered the chamber away from matters raised by the victims – the rapes, the treatment in the camps – since neither the defence nor even the prosecution seemed to have an interest in bringing these issues forward. In time, the victims and their representatives were moved firmly to the sidelines.

It was not until 9 December 2009, seven months after the victims submitted the petition, that the Appeals Chamber handed down its decision. No one was surprised to learn the majority decision was overturned and the petition rejected. There would be no modification of the charges and no discussion of sexual slavery in the camps or the brutal treatment of the young people kept there. The text of the Appeals Chamber decision was a tortuous path through arguments about procedure, about what each of the submissions meant or could mean, about the primacy of statute articles over regulations. In fact, it had little to do with whether the chamber could consider new elements of a crime once the trial was underway, even though this had been the original query and more to do with whether the majority decision had been argued properly. There was not a word anywhere about Ituri or the substance of the case.

The failure of the petition showed how far removed the chamber was from the occurrences in central Africa, a chamber that seemed week by week to have little stomach for the criminal court's actual stock-in-trade, assigning responsibility for the misfortunes suffered in a chaotic war. There were exceptions, certainly, but these were curiously few. The victims had brought the turbulence of the Congo in too close for the comfort of those who preferred to proceed by measured steps under the regimen of procedures, under rules and manners, and under the judge's square authority, with the counsellors skirting daintily around an issue in euphemistic language. As an observer, I often had the sense I was in the middle of a charade, a dancing around the real subject so as not to offend the sensibilities of the law or the judge, who was ever ready to bring the trial to a halt if something irritated him.

Luc Walleyn, the esteemed Belgian attorney-at-law, was one of the victims' legal representatives. En route to his office in Brussels, the taxi driver said knowingly when I gave the address, "I know this *quartier*. These are my people. I am Turkish. And look, that statue – Ataturk. Great man." He explained how Romanians had later moved in and, sure they get along with them, and then the Africans moved in, and you might think people here don't get along. We do. We help each other. He pointed in passing to a sign in Romanian, turned up a small one-way street and around a corner, down another one-way street and up a small hill. I asked if he knew the way.

"You think I don't know the place. I know it. That lawyer's not my personal friend. He's a lawyer right, but this place says a lot, and if he's got his place here, he's different from the others. Has to be."

We came to a simple residential facade with a small brass plaque announcing here was a lawyer's *cabinet*.

The driver waited till someone came to the door, then gave a thumbs up.

"Come in," said a kindly elderly woman as she helped me through the narrow vestibule.

"There," she said, "your coat."

"Yes, well he is expecting you, but if you will wait a few minutes … There's no one with him, just he's preparing some notes. He likes quiet for this. Would you like something?" she asked in French. "Tea?"

"No thanks."

"Really, it's no problem."

It was only a few moments before Luc Walleyn opened the door to his office, smiling warmly. To begin with, he spoke of the neighbourhood. It suited him. He had moved here because of the people, who were congenial and not distant as the burghers of downtown Brussels could be.

He had been a law student at Louvain University in the late sixties when political sensibilities were alive, in Paris as the students of May 1968 peppered the police with cobblestones, and in New York as students blockaded classrooms at Columbia University. He had

joined the marches in the streets of Brussels and, in time, his awareness grew about those who needed help, not just with the law but
with justice itself. In Brussels, these were the immigrants, the first-
generation Moroccans and Turks and Lebanese who had come seeking refuge and languished in the streets, confined by dislocation and
racism. When he qualified for the law, he gravitated to their plight,
and the more he listened to them and represented them in court, the
more he was drawn to open an office in their neighbourhood.

His early cases had been difficult. He told me about one of an
African girl living in Belgium who had been forced in her home
country to marry a man against her will; in her struggle to avoid
deportation she spent time in jail, and at one point she was suffocated to death by a policeman. The Human Rights League asked
him to prosecute the police charged with her murder. He did.
There was the case of the Belgian peacekeepers charged with racist
behaviour while serving in Mogadishu; he took that case as well.
He developed a reputation for defending the defenceless, the victims. He became a mainstay of Avocats sans frontières – Lawyers
without Borders – to bring legal services to victims who had no
other possibility for defending themselves. Some members supported the organization but charged for their services, and Lubanga's
counsel, Maître Mabille, was one. She worked for the accused. Not
he. He chose to defend victims, and the victims of Lubanga chose
him as one of the lawyers representing them. He was the only non-
African among them.

"The problem with the case against Lubanga was the prosecution let the trial go forward on a very narrow basis," he said.

He was not sure why this had happened, except perhaps that it
made it easier for the prosecutor to win. But it did nothing for the
victims and no one should have been surprised at their petition.
Letting the trial continue on such narrow charges might have served
Lubanga, it was more comfortable for the judge, and perhaps it
served the interests of the prosecution as well. But not Ituri and
not the victims. Not really anyone outside of the chamber. It was
apparent to him that having victims in the chamber disturbed the
balance between the accused on one side and the accusers on the

other, since the victims were raw evidence against the accused and would weigh in powerfully against Lubanga. It was a problem certainly for Maître Mabille and her defence, and of course she stood firmly opposed. The judge? The trial chamber was his bailiwick where he kept things under a controlling hand. Having victims in his chamber actively involved in the proceedings simply made things too messy for the judge.

Everyone knew there had been sexual slavery and inhumane treatment of the children in the camps under Lubanga's command. Luc Walleyn smiled as he recalled the exchange in the chamber. He had reminded the Court that the victims, his clients, sought to broaden the charges as a matter of principle, and indeed if the chamber refused to literally broaden the charges, the chamber should at least open these crimes for discussion as aggravating elements. Why worry, he had asked the court, if the chamber heard evidence that Lubanga's men had systematically raped young girls? The judge could consider the discussion at his discretion. It seemed sensible enough. But Judge Fulford would not allow it. He seemed sure that if he allowed a modification of the charges, the trial would have to start over. Judge Fulford had posed the question to Luc Walleyn in the courtroom: did he not agree that discussing new crimes would alter the trial irreparably and force them to go back to the beginning? Of course not, Walleyn had replied. The formalities of procedure should not stand in the way of laying out the facts of the case. If Thomas Lubanga and his commanders had enslaved young girls for their pleasure or shot young boys in the head to teach others discipline, this was part of the case, no matter how it came before the court.

When the Appeals Chamber rejected the petition, Luc Walleyn knew the question was closed for good. Whenever the discussion turned to the rape of young girls, as it did from time to time, or when someone urged the Court to consider something not formally covered by the charges, Judge Fulford made a point of saying the issue was settled. No one doubted that limiting the charges served the convenience of the chamber more than the interests of justice, but that, Luc Walleyn said with a smile, is what happened.

Did he think there would be any damage to the Court's reputation from all this, I asked him as we rose and walked towards the door?

He hesitated.

Let's remember, he said, this was the first case. Everyone was on trial, not just Lubanga. One thing we know is the law looks after itself first. The prosecution wanted a conviction. The defence wanted a light sentence. And the judge wanted to get things over with. They all got what they wanted.

The judge's indifference to the victims would haunt the case. There was a good chance Lubanga would be acquitted, abandoning the victims to their fate in Ituri in the wake of the trial. Even if Lubanga were convicted on the charge of recruiting children as soldiers, the few victims who had proof that they had been child soldiers might find recompense, but the majority of others – those who had been victims of sexual violence or theft or other criminal acts – would be dismissed. In any case, they received almost no attention in the course of the trial, and that meant they would get even less attention afterwards when it really counted.

It would have been a very different trial had the victims figured more in the proceedings, something measurably closer to the Rome Statute's vision. Listening to the victims would have forced the Chamber to consider the real breadth of Lubanga's crimes, not just those chosen for strategic purposes. It would have committed the Chamber to speak openly about how the boys and girls were treated in the camps, and not just their recruitment. But there was something even more fundamental. It would have shifted the focus from the parlour game of who was to prevail in the case to doing what it took to restore social stability in Ituri by offering recompense to those who had suffered. Reparations would have been at least something to keep in mind and not just an afterthought.[3] This would have shown Ituri and the international community that the Court was fulfilling its promise not just to address individual crimes but their social consequences as well.

chapter 12

Lies, All Lies

I first heard about Alec Wargo while trying to uncover the routes the rebels in the Eastern Congo took to smuggle gold out and use their profits to buy arms. Those who knew the Eastern Congo said Wargo would know if anyone would. He was a young American living in Uvira, a forlorn Congolese town at the southern tip of Lake Tanganyika, one of the places where precious metals were funnelled out of the country on small boats crossing the lake into Tanzania to be sold to brokers in Mombasa. He had come to know most of the warlords and rebel leaders in the area, though not because of the gold; he was hanging out with them, getting their confidence in hopes he could in time get them to release the child soldiers from their small militias and let them go home.

He had joined the UN's child protection section after university, and though he might have chosen a more conventional career, he opted instead for an entry job caring for kids caught up in the Congo wars. He kept track of them, found ways to help. He wore a healthy American grin and a polo shirt as he walked from one warlord's compound to the next, glad-handing, chit-chatting, cruising without hesitation through heavily guarded compounds or camps where he found children curled up around their Kalashnikovs. I visited him there to see how he put his chutzpah to work in documenting the derelictions of Congolese rebels. He once marched into the house of a local warlord undaunted and there – beckoning me to follow – put his notebook on the table, joking all the while with a man who had committed a legion of violent crimes.

In early 2004 in the wake of Ituri's upheaval, the United Nations asked Alec to take over child protection in Ituri for an interim period. Fighting had stopped in the city of Bunia by that time but not in the rural expanse of Ituri, where the warlords had gone with their armies and their supplies and their *kadogos*, and where there were still skirmishes between Lubanga's Hema and Floribert Ngabu's Lendu and others. Alec found their encampments. He visited one after the other, counting the kids under their command. It was a dangerous task moving from one bush camp to the next, but he did it, and even though the worst of the wars was over, he found the number of children under one military command or another was higher than anyone imagined. His report told how many and why. Some might quibble about the age of the children he saw and how he knew who was a child and who was not and what proof he had, but the truth was Alec had spent his share of time looking at Congolese kids. He may have misjudged a few, but this was hardly an issue when the child soldiers he found numbered in the thousands. After adding up all the *kadogos* under Lubanga and Kakwavu and Kahwa Panga at Mandro and the few still under Nyamwisi, he estimated more than ten thousand in Ituri at the time, three thousand under Lubanga's command alone.

Alec asked as many as he could what kept them there. Were they there to protect their ethnic groups or did they even care about that? Did they hope to avenge the deaths of their mothers and fathers or the destruction of their homes? Some gave these reasons, of course, though not many. They were there because their homes were long gone, the war had wreaked havoc on their lives, and it might even have been their commanders Kisembo or Kakwavu or Chief Kahwa Panga whose men had murdered their mothers and fathers and set the kids adrift, but still they were here under their command because they had nowhere else to go. Alec's 2004 report on child soldiers in Ituri was written before Lubanga was arrested and well before the trial had begun and was without any intent to incriminate Lubanga, or anyone else for that matter. It was simply a factual account, and it was only when he learned of my interest in the trial many years later that he offered to dig up the document. "Enjoy," he said in the e-mail subject line. I put it in the satchel I was carrying en route to Paris to meet with the estimable Maître Mabille and it was still in my bag on the morning I sat opposite her.

"Child soldiers? It's a fabrication," Mabille said. "Not one of the witnesses is who they say they are. They are liars, all liars."

In 1912 there was a strange archaeological discovery in the Piltdown gravel pit in south-central England, and though it had nothing to do with war crimes or child soldiers, there was something about that discovery that is pertinent to the Lubanga trial. The find was an anomaly. It was a skull that the respected paleo-archaeologists of the time decided, after due consideration, was none other than the missing link, half-man-half-ape bridging the divide between humans and primates. It did not seem to matter much to the eminent scientists that there were grave suspicions about the skull, for the shape was decidedly unlikely: a cranium nearly the size of a modern human's and a mandible that belonged to an ape. Here it was, nevertheless, a new piece of the fossil record, and it was to be noted that this celebrated missing link had been an Englishman.

Forty-one years passed before Piltdown Man was officially declared a deception. Someone had planted the skull in the gravel pit – probably one of the paleo-archaeologists who discovered it and brought it to the public's attention – spurred on by ambition and by the desire for notoriety and perhaps some sort of a patriotic satisfaction that the very first human, if there could be such a thing, walked proudly on English soil. The strange skull had been pieced together from fragments, a human cranium and the jaw of an orang-utan, to give the illusion that there had been a creature – however unlikely – with a developed brain and the jaw of a chimp. The evidence was false, a conspiracy of ambitious paleo-archaeologists. And still, in spite of all the doubts and misgivings, it entered the scientific canon for more than four decades, just as Maître Mabille's claim entered in all seriousness the trial's body of evidence that in fact there was no bona fide evidence of child soldiers serving under Lubanga in Ituri.

Like scientific procedures, court procedures are governed by measures for protecting what is known about a case from being captured by special interests or by calculated deceit. Sources are checked, witnesses interrogated, documents verified, and informers protected, all to ensure that the information reaches the Chamber free of contamination. The judges go through their protocols, the registry does what it can to allow witnesses to speak without fear of reprisals, and the Court purges the examination environment of all circumstances that might somehow lead a witness to misrepresent the truth and taint what judges and bystanders and counsellors come to know. Courts operate under the assumption that only in exceptional cases do untruths make their way into the record.

But they did. When Maître Mabille went fiercely on the offensive, beginning early in the trial, it was first dismissed as a healthy check on the prosecution's claims. Then she struck out ever more boldly, questioning the most obvious facts about the case and did not rest there; it was no longer a date here or there, or the year a witness attended school that was covered with suspicion. She insisted every witness had an ulterior motive and every investigator was conspiring with lies and more lies.

The bold strategy of the defence was to convince the Chamber that the prosecution's entire edifice of evidence was rotten throughout. At the top of the conspiracy pyramid was the prosecutor who, as far as Maître Mabille was concerned, was out to make a name for himself, using the trial to grandstand while caring little about reputable legal practice. At the bottom of the information supply chain were the child soldiers themselves and the Congolese informants who had had contact with them in the demobilization centres and worked with the prosecution to bring them to The Hague. It was also everyone in between. There were the child soldiers looking for a way to milk the Court for some advantage; there were the parents of the witnesses and their uncles and aunts angling to get something out of the Court or perhaps use the court to discredit their enemies; there were even the experts with their own interests, though it was hard to fathom why these experts would want something for themselves by massaging their testimony. As Maître Mabille saw it, untruths were everywhere.

One could not help wondering how it could be, whether there might be some explanation for why it was so easy for Maître Mabille to use a scattering of inconsistencies to conclude that everyone from top to bottom was telling half-truths. To be sure, sticking strictly to the truth was a lesser moral imperative for Iturians as they struggled to reclaim their lives after the violence of 2002 and 2003; for many Iturians desperate to restore some stability in their lives, there was a lot to hide. Hedging the truth made some sense in these times, and one had to accept that there would be lies in testimonies as there were in real life. But that did not begin to justify the issue that was made of them or to excuse the grievous decision the judge made in assuming that one half-truth was enough to discredit everything a witness said.

Truths and lies in the Lubanga courtroom all make more sense when seen as an extension of the lives and times of Ituri after the fighting in 2003, once the armed groups had left town. Bunia changed rapidly. Peacekeepers could be seen in the streets with their Land Cruisers. The patio of Le Hellenique on the main street that had gone silent during the fighting came back to life with the return of foreigners. Its Greek owners could be seen standing outside with their hands on their hips, looking up and down the street. The airport came back to life. Foreign agencies and NGOs from different parts of the world were rushing in with their modest sums to give relief.

The United Nations Children Fund brought in their infant feeding programs. The United Nations Development Program set up peace-building projects in towns from Bunia to Aru to Fataki. Incentives were offered for those still in armed groups to surrender their arms in exchange for training in a trade. Some organizations had a mandate to help women, while others were there to assist those injured in the wars. Others were there expressly to work with child soldiers. There was money and clothes on offer for the child soldiers, the *kadogos*, and cash to pay for their schooling as long as they could prove they had fought in the wars and could hand in a gun. A fledgling market emerged for those looking for a piece of the post-war peace-building funds.

Getting help from any of them was always a negotiation. The organizations had to believe that applicants were right for their cause. If someone served in the army, that was an asset, and there were hopefuls who had served but maybe not in the right way to qualify. They might have to change their story about who they were or what happened to meet a certain requirement. If a young man came in who claimed to be a soldier but had no gun to give up, he would have to make up a story to explain it. Parents might inflate the number of their children they care for to get more from a feeding program. Some looking for a place in a woodworking program might claim experience that they never had. These were half-truths, all of them, and all of them necessities of life in post-war Ituri. A boy soldier who had been contacted by someone from the International Criminal Court would not hesitate to claim he was younger than he really was, just to make his own case stronger.

I met a young man from the small town of Fataki who had settled in Bunia when the fighting was over. Following an entrepreneur's program, he received a portion of the 110 dollars on offer to make his transition out of the army into civilian life. He drafted a plan to start a barbershop. Some of his money was used for learning to cut hair; he was serious, since he had no interest in returning to his armed group demanding tolls from travellers at roadblocks. While waiting for the rest of the money he would use to rent a real shop, he set up a stall on the side of the road to serve a few passersby, though he knew they would never be enough. He waited and waited for the money to come for his shop with his simple straight-back chair on the side of the road, getting a pittance from one or two customers a day.

At first, anything seemed better than his previous life, roaming the countryside with armed gangs raiding villages, living off stolen goats and the small reserves of grain they could grab. But the money for his shop never came. He visited another transit centre to see if there was anything. He lied to them that he did not have a gun to hand in as it was lost and said he had not received help from any other agency. He made up a new name for himself in case they kept records somewhere. He claimed his parents were dead, and that was a lie.

The young man with barber ambitions never did get the money for his shop, and one day he disappeared into his old armed group to raze villages and steal goats. There were dozens like him. Some received training and were lucky enough to find work. A very few made their way, with the help of NGO workers at the transit centres, to the Offices of the International Criminal Court outside of Bunia and agreed to be witnesses in the case against Lubanga. Working for the Court was risky, but they were young men and women in an unsure world, without food or parents or places to stay, with little more to their name than the accounts they could conjure; all they had to give was their testimony. For many of them, truth had become a liability. There was nothing wrong if they embellished the reasons that brought them there. It meant there were lies, though not because the witnesses had something to hide, as Maître Mabille presumed, or because they were inveterate prevaricators but simply because they were trying to recover a life lost to war.

In post-war Ituri, the primary concern was survival. People did things they would not have done in more normal circumstances, in order to stay alive. They joined an army and quit. They joined a different army and quit again. They took more than their share of food rations if they could and lied about it. They might have killed someone and lied about that. It was a privilege if you could afford to be honest, though most people could not and most everyone was forced, however disgraceful it was, to tell half-truths as a way of making the best of a bad situation.

This allowed Maître Mabille and the defence counsellors to proceed undeterred and made her wholesale depiction of all Iturians as liars the harder to challenge. She built her case upon these wartime liberties that people took with the truth to undermine the credibility of those who took the stand. That meant there were fierce odds against any witness who took the stand seeking only to tell the truth of wartime in Ituri.

Like so many of the child soldiers who testified, Mercimungu ran the risk of retaliation. The danger was pervasive and touched every aspect of the trial, from the protection schemes to the layout of the courtroom, from the press coverage to the redaction of trial transcripts. Lubanga and his family were powerful in Ituri, and there was no force strong enough to protect anyone who dared to say something against him, even if this something was no more than admitting to being a child soldier. The most vulnerable of all were the Hema boys and girls, themselves members of Lubanga's family or living in his neighbourhood, because their testimony was not just disloyal, it was a betrayal. And the closer in kinship a young person was to Lubanga himself, the more danger there was: his family knew your family, his brothers knew your parents, and the life of your parents was as much in jeopardy as your own. Mercimungu's family members were all Hema and lived in the neighbourhood of Lubanga's immediate kin.

He had not joined up willingly. He had been abducted from school at age thirteen or fourteen, when Lubanga's troopers stormed into his school room and began seizing children and herding them with sticks into the back of two trucks. The troopers carted the children to Camp Mandro, a place for training the children, and threw them into mud-and-wattle shacks, where they had to sleep on top of one another and suffer the harsh discipline from older boys. Mercimungu could not stand it at first; after a few days he ran away through the forests to the road and along the road all night to the house of his mother and father, only to discover when he arrived home that they would not have him. There had been threats from their Hema neighbours. He would have to return to the camp.

He endured. He went through the training and was assigned to a group stopping vehicles along a road extorting money and food. He was a thoughtful boy, he questioned things, and once when his group stopped a UNICEF truck carrying rations for poor families, the UNICEF man asked him why was he doing this, and from that moment on, he saw things differently. He considered leaving the army many times but never did, for fear of what would happen to his mother and father. As time went on, though, he saw more clearly the wrong that was being done and the wrong done to him. Two years later, when the investigators for the Office of the Prosecution arrived in Bunia looking for witnesses to testify against Lubanga, he said he would.

He knew the perils. The brother of Thomas Lubanga himself personally warned Mercimungu what could happen to him. He was frightened at first. As the time approached for Mercimungu to depart for The Hague, the threats from Lubanga's kin became more ominous. The brother called a meeting of the neighbourhood where Mercimungu lived and where his parents lived, and he pointed the finger at anyone who had been in touch with the Office of the Prosecution. His finger singled out Mercimungu. In front of neighbours and relatives, Lubanga's kinsman told him that if he went to The Hague he was to say he had never been a child soldier. He was to say he had never carried a weapon and he had been bribed to come to the Court. There was no doubt what the brother was also saying: anyone who testified at the trial against Lubanga and who helped the prosecution convict him would be hunted down.

The same thing happened to his cousins and friends from the neighbourhood who were all in the meeting. Afterwards, most of them decided it was too risky to testify. Some of them even agreed to join up with the defence to discredit the prosecution's case, saying they had been paid to lie about being child soldiers. One or two of them agreed to go to The Hague and say this in the trial. This made them into heroes at home instead of traitors, and even Mercimungu, shortly before he left for The Hague, went to meet with the defence under pressure. But he knew even then what his decision would be; he had made up his mind to tell the truth, in spite of the fact he was beleaguered from all sides: from the defence who called him a liar, from his father who barred him from the house, and from his neighbourhood that labelled him a traitor.

Mercimungu would never have dared to face his family's disapproval, nor would he have passed the repeated interrogations with the prosecution's investigators if in fact he was not telling the truth about being a child soldier. The judge, however, was persuaded by the defence that Mercimungu was lying, that he was an impostor like all the others. The judge drew on some curious evidence provided by the defence: a piece of paper from the school he attended showing that he was registered in school at the time when he claimed to be in the army, though no one could explain how that happened. The judge concluded that Mercimungu's account "overall, is unreliable. It is likely that the intermediary persuaded or encouraged him to give false evidence. The Chamber is unable to rely on his account."

That was final. The Court decided Mercimungu could not be considered a child soldier, a highly improbable conclusion. Evidence had become so murky with claims and counterclaims, accusations and counter-accusations that even the most obvious of truths could be discounted as counterfeit. And no one in the Chamber commanded enough judgment or respect to set the record right.

The Chamber came to be firmly possessed by a notion so deeply unlikely that it strained credibility. How could it be that all of the young child soldier witnesses were liars? Everyone knew there had been large numbers of them. Even if the young men and women who appeared before the Court had been chosen at random, it would have been unusual if none had been child soldiers. But they were not chosen at random. They had been screened by the investigators and vetted by the prosecution, and still the Chamber, the judge, and Maître Mabille could conclude that none of them were and that the charges against Lubanga were fabrications. For those attentive to the substance of the trial it seemed that such a strange conclusion could hardly help but collapse under the weight of its own preposterousness.

And yet it did not.

As the trial stumbled on, the scandal of the go-betweens, the intermediaries, who had, according to the defence, coached the witnesses on what to say, mushroomed until it consumed the trial entirely. The Court commissioned a study on the role of these intermediaries and their associated witnesses to review every instance when an intermediary supposedly persuaded a witness to give false testimony. It was the lead up to a demand by the defence to bring the intermediaries to The Hague to testify in public. Maître Mabille knew well the prosecution would try to stop her, for the prosecution had earlier refused to allow the identities of the intermediaries to be public. But by this time – and given the favour Maître Mabille held in the Chamber – the prosecution had no choice. Discord grew. The crimes of Lubanga were now crowded out by the cacophony of complaints against the prosecution and the refrain of the defence that the prosecution was basing its case on a tissue of lies. Relations in the courtroom were ugly and they were about to get uglier.

chapter 13

Under the Judge's Skin

Judge Fulford could by turns be learned, gregarious, stern, and funny, even harsh at times, depending on the circumstances. He was almost never out of sorts. The prosecutor's distaste for what he saw as the judge's pretentiousness did cause him to chafe occasionally, but even when the prosecutor was at his most irritating, the judge never lost his cool, and in fact no one ever really sent him off his rails. Except one: Béatrice le Fraper du Hellen. She was disarmingly charming and gracious, a ranking French diplomat reputed for her expertise in human rights law and, during the Lubanga trial, on loan to the International Criminal Court as a deputy prosecutor and head of the Jurisdiction, Complementarity, and Cooperation Division. She got under the judge's skin with nothing more than an interview.

Relations in the Chamber were strained anyway from the tension building in February and March 2010 as the defence argued with increasing vehemence that the intermediaries had corrupted evidence by persuading witnesses to lie. Maître Mabille's defence team took the slightest discrepancies in the testimonies as evidence of the nefarious influence of the intermediaries. The idea was to convince the Chamber that after locating witnesses for the trial, the prosecution's intermediaries had then instructed the witnesses about what they should say when they got to Court. It was never clear what the motivation might have been for the intermediaries to push the witnesses to lie, or whether there really was a conspiracy, as the defence claimed, to pervert the evidence, or how it might have given the Chamber the wrong impression of what actually happened. The plan to accuse the intermediaries of perverting evidence had little to do with the facts of the case, since these were widely known, and it made little sense to dispute Lubanga's recruitment of underage children. Its real purpose was to discredit the witnesses, the intermediaries, and, in turn, the prosecution.

Labelling intermediaries as deliberate deceivers would have seemed frivolous had the defence not pressed the matter heavily upon the Chamber and with the judge's approval. Only one of the prosecution's witnesses complained about being coached, and he later changed his story. No matter. The defence was constructing an argument by bringing in young men and women of their own choosing ready to testify that they had been in contact with the prosecution through intermediaries who, they said, wanted them to lie. Some of them were from Lubanga's neighbourhood who had come into the defence's camp in hopes of protecting themselves and their families. They testified before the Chamber that the intermediaries had asked them to lie about birthdates, about the battles they fought and the schools they went to.

The momentum of the trial was shifting in favour of Maître Mabille and, seizing the moment, she went even more determinedly on the attack. She pushed the prosecution into a pitched battle. She would demand an audience with the intermediaries, knowing the prosecution would have to oppose her, having promised the intermediaries to keep their identity secret. She would insist on putting them on the stand. By March 2010 the defence had insisted the main intermediaries should appear before the Court in full view of whoever was watching the trial, and the Office of the Prosecution was powerless to stop her. The prosecution forwarded reasoned submissions to the Chamber; they offered to condense the information made available by the intermediaries and provide them to the defence. They delayed where they could. None of it made any difference. Maître Mabille insisted that, no matter what the consequences were, the intermediaries would have to take the stand.

⁓

Béatrice le Fraper du Hellen's interview with Mr Wairagala Wabaki had been arranged for 15 March. It was nothing particularly out of the ordinary. Mr Wairagala was chronicling the trial for the Open Society Institute, and because his regular reports were even-handed, he became the go-to spokesperson for the Lubanga case. He sent his interviewee, Ms Le Fraper du Hellen, the questions in advance, and it was no surprise the first of them asked whether she knew the intermediaries.

Of course she knew them. There were not many, seven or eight, though only four main ones, and she knew them all, except perhaps the one who had come to the prosecution from the Congolese Agence Nationale de Renseignement, the state intelligence service stationed in Bunia. The others were NGO types, social workers, activists, and human rights advocates. Most of the intermediaries had worked in the transit centres helping child soldiers who had been caught up in the wars, taking care of them when they demobilized, and helping them find their parents if they could. They practised their commitment to social justice.

"They are in the news these days," she said, "because the defence has made it their strategy to make them look bad. The intermediaries are committed to their own jobs, they are supportive of international justice and we are careful about who we choose."

She was asked then if she thought the judge would protect their identity as the prosecution had hoped.

"At this stage, no."

"The defence," she said, "they don't like what the child soldiers are saying, so they are telling us maybe those child soldiers were influenced. And I am saying we have very courageous, very brave child soldiers who have managed to make a life after what they have suffered. The defence are making the trial about the intermediaries, but it is really about child soldiers."

She spoke about how the defence's fixation on intermediaries had made child soldiers almost irrelevant. She wanted to correct this if she could, though it was difficult, and she knew it was difficult to bring up the damage done to child soldiers as long as there was a succession of defence witnesses complaining loudly about the intermediaries.

"Some people are buying whatever the defence is saying. I am saying the opposite: intermediaries are just what they are – intermediaries. In this case, they are none other than, well, fantastic and committed people."

Mr Wairagala Wabaki asked her about the protection for the witnesses. Was it enough? Would it ever be enough? Did she have anything to say about that?

She did, though she knew there was not much she could say to counter the objections the defence had repeatedly raised about protection measures. The prosecution had done what they could to protect their witnesses from the possibilities of retaliation, though she knew, as others knew, the protection measures could go only so far. Blinds and vocal distortion were no more than a partial remedy for helping the young witnesses with the fear they felt when they entered the courtroom.

"Our witnesses," she said, "many of them are Hema children. It is a pity but they are still considered by most of Hema society as traitors. I regret it, you regret it, we all regret it, but that's the way it is, so they have to be protected, their identity has to be protected. And imagine, Lubanga knows who they are and frankly I am amazed at the courage of the children. They actually were in the courtroom with Lubanga, and you know, Mr Lubanga, he is making signs to the audience, he is smiling, and he is doing a lot of body language – it is terrifying for the children to testify in front of him."

And what about the intermediaries? How far would the prosecution go in protecting them? If the prosecution tried to protect their identity, there was the risk of an application by the defence midway through the case that the trial should be stayed as an abuse of process. And the judge would probably agree. It had happened before.

"There is," she answered perfunctorily, "absolutely no abuse of process. Prosecutor Moreno-Ocampo is a very accurate and fair prosecutor and, as I have said, whatever the case the defence has, it was built by Prosecutor Moreno-Ocampo based on the evidence gathered by the prosecution. So this is just talk."

"I understand why the defence are going after the intermediaries," she said. "It is obvious. It's their last chance, but nothing is going to happen. Mr Lubanga is going away for a long time."

⁓

The interview appeared on 15 March 2010.[1] Two days later, on a Wednesday morning, the court usher in Chamber One pronounced "All rise," and once again the judges filed in and took their places. Judge Fulford skipped his usual niceties. He was displeased.

"I'm conscious," said the judge, addressing the counsellor for the prosecution, "of the well-worn adage that one should not shoot the messenger, but you will no doubt have read the interview given two days ago by someone of the name of Béatrice Le Fraper du Hellen."

There was a palpable shift in atmosphere.

"I want your assistance in relation to that interview. A theme throughout – now let me quote – is that the intermediaries are 'very committed persons, very supportive of international justice. We are very careful about who we choose as intermediaries.'" Here the judge paused briefly. "This is not an off-the-cuff remark but a theme of the interview, presumably on the basis of firm and substantial evidence that the intermediaries are very committed persons who are very supportive of international justice."

"I am unaware," he continued, "of any evidence that has been served by the prosecution in line with those very clear and unequivocal indications."

The judge peered disapprovingly at the counsellor for the prosecution.

"Then there is this: 'But nothing is going to happen. Mr Lubanga is going away for a long time.'"

The more the judge was perturbed, the more he spoke in stilted legalese.

"My question to you is this: since when has it been for the prosecutor or his representative to determine what the result of this trial is going to be, should the accused be convicted, whether or not he is going to receive a short, an intermediate, or a long sentence? And do you think it is appropriate for the prosecutor, midway through the trial, through his representative, to be telling the public and the judges what the result is going to be of the trial over which we are presiding?"

He did not wait for an answer.

"The next issue I wish to have your assistance on is this. I think the Rome Statute unamended still leaves the Bench in the position of deciding on what facts are or are not proven in this case. If I am wrong on that, I would like your guidance please, but there are observations by Ms Le Fraper du Hellen which seem to indicate that the prosecutor is of the view it is for him to determine what facts are proven."

His mien was dour. The ramparts of his authority had been breached. No one, as far as he was concerned, neither from the prosecution nor from the press nor from those sitting in the gallery, had the liberty to infringe on his sovereignty in the Chamber. The suggestion that Mr Lubanga was intimidating witnesses grated on him particularly.

"I want to see copies, please, of the videos in which the prosecutor himself is alleging that this has occurred. Because if it is to be suggested that we have been allowing the accused, through his actions, to terrify prosecution witnesses, that is to allege that the three of us [the three judges] have not been discharging our functions properly."

Of course there were no videos or any evidence to show the intermediaries were either fantastic or committed; nor would Béatrice le Fraper du Hellen justify with hard evidence her speculation about what would happen to Lubanga. The judge knew that. He was posturing and to a purpose: to quarantine the trial under his exclusive authority from observers and commentators like Ms Béatrice le Fraper du Hellen and other members of the public concerned with the trial.

"Finally, Ms Samson, you might like to remind Béatrice le Fraper du Hellen that a very considerable time ago, when we were considering the whole issue of witness summaries and what was to be published in the press, I gave a very firm indication that the judges did not expect to see satellite litigation in the press, with the issues which we are considering being the subject of some kind of debate, with commentators on one or both sides seeking to litigate the issues in this trial in a different forum. This is not an appropriate activity."

He made it clear that this was not a trial for the public. Open commentary was not welcome.[2]

~

The tandem commitment of the International Criminal Court to justice and to the larger purposes of peace is ingrained in the Rome Statute. The Preamble to the Rome Statute makes the unambiguous claim that "such grave crimes threaten the peace, security and well-being of the world." Therein lies the Court's commitment to reduce conflict. Punishing crimes and advancing peace go hand-in-hand.

This dual assignment bothers some scholars of the law. Some find it wrong-headed to bring peace-building into the judicial domain, peace being one thing and justice another. Some think it should do one or the other, hand out either retributive or restorative justice, not both.[3] Some have gone so far as to say it interferes with peace negotiations by pulling key parties, guilty that they may be, out of the negotiations to stand trial on their own; it leaves peace negotiations stranded. When in 2005 the Court issued arrest warrants for five members of the rapacious Lord's Resistance Army in Northern Uganda, critics objected because the government of Uganda had just promised amnesty for those who might otherwise have come forward to join the reconciliation process.[4] Some even claimed that it was the arrest warrant for Joseph Kony, the leader of the Lord's Resistance Army, that kept him in hiding and made peace impossible.

Joseph Kony was a madman, but he was no fool. We now know that he would never have come forward under any circumstances, arrest warrant or not. The dichotomy between peace and justice so frequently debated by academics has rarely been more than a red herring. The problem is really finding ways for a court, deeply steeped in juridical procedures, to broaden its function to integrate peace-building with adjudication. And there is the rub. Litigators and judges would rather not be bothered with obligations outside of the legal box, even though there are some simple things the Court can do to pacify tensions in the places where crimes are committed.

The Court can invite commentary, rather than shun it, as Judge Fulford did. It can demonstrate that it is acting in the interests of the common weal, the victims and the populace at large, by keeping the trial open to public scrutiny instead of closing off dialogue. This is a critical step in bringing peace and justice together. But Judge Fulford wanted to cordon off the trial from public debate. He might have feared that an open dialogue with the public would derail debates in the Chamber even further.

Ituri's conflict between Lubanga's Hema aggressors and their victims was recreated in the courtroom. This is inevitable in war crimes. There are always risks that old enmities will be reawakened. But there are advantages here as well. Re-enacting a grievance in the presence of a mediator or counsellor or judge can dissipate the animus that lies in the bitter hearts of the victims. It was quite possible that in a more conciliatory courtroom, and with a judge more given to airing grievances than abetting the contest that inspired violent acts in the first place, the tenor of the courtroom might have been different. It might have allowed a more honest appraisal of the crimes for which Lubanga was responsible. Other reconciliation projects have succeeded in doing this in Ituri. Informal courts to settle land disputes between rival parties after the war in Ituri have done this in different parts of the region. Village-level women's peace committees have also done this. The trial itself, with its international stature and with the authority that the Court brought to matters in Ituri, could have done this too with real effect but only had the judge pulled the curtains aside on the Chamber's deliberation to let others be witness to Lubanga's rampage. The Chamber did not do that. Instead of drawing open the curtains, the judge drew them closed to the extent he was able.

Béatrice Le Fraper du Hellen's common sense interview might have been a step in that direction. It was conciliatory enough. It was candid and sufficiently without guile to allow a moment of uncontested exchange within the Chamber. But the judge saw no reason for any of that. Better to vilify Béatrice le Fraper du Hellen as an interloper than to allow her to air her candid views of the character of the intermediaries and the genuine suffering of the child soldiers. If the public at large was to see anything of the evidence or to reflect on the wages of war crimes, the judge preferred it to be through his own lens. It was for him and him alone, free of any other commentary or outside intervention, to decide whether intermediaries were decent people who could perhaps be believed, or whether, as he seemed to suspect, they were villainous liars whose role in the trial had been to falsify testimony, their own and others', through and through.

In the days following the interview, the judge seemed strangely flummoxed by this woman's intervention. He would raise it impromptu from time to time as he mused out loud what she could possibly mean by this or that. She dogged him for the more than two years remaining in the trial.

Some regarded her interview as a turning point, where the judge finally resolved to give little quarter henceforth to the prosecutor. I could not help wondering what kind of woman might have left so indelible a mark. Within weeks of her interview, Béatrice le Fraper du Hellen had left the Office of the Prosecutor in The Hague and had taken a post with the French Permanent Mission to the United Nations in New York. Her sudden departure was no doubt out of necessity. Sometime later I asked if she would agree to speak with me about the trial, wondering all the while whether unpleasant associations might still linger from the verbal drubbing she had taken from the judge.

She agreed. I fully expected her to be a ministry official attired in foreign service grey, gracious throughout, and probably unwilling to speak about the Lubanga trial, where her own comments had sparked such a storm. I anticipated an office that would be a labyrinth of protocol. When I arrived at her New York office late in the day, I was informed she was held up in a meeting, with the characteristic assurances that she would be only a brief minute or two. I was shown to a chair outside the office suites and waited while minutes passed. The more time passed, the more I prepared myself for a firm woman with dark hair pinned securely down, gracious to a fault, and sorry for the delay, asking for my understanding that her busy schedule permitted only a few short moments.

Suddenly a free-wheeling effusive blond woman burst through the doors with her hands together namaste-style ohmygod, ohmygod … you don't mind, she said. Come! Come! My office will do. She rushed to find plastic cups for a half-glass of frosty green tea poured from a near-empty corner store jug. Her hair was flyaway, not dark or pinned down, and she was not by any stretch the shrew demonized by the judge. She wore an animal print vest and a flowing skirt, she warned me she would tell me anything I wanted to know, and with that she fell into a chair in front of her desk, took a deep breath, and smiled broadly in my direction.

"We all worked as a team," she said, "the Office of the Prosecution."

"That interview," she said, "had not been impromptu, it was planned. It was not something out of the blue. We should have done more of this sort of thing from the beginning."

"After the first year, the defence had all of us in the Office of the Prosecution in a corner and turned our witnesses and our staff in Ituri into liars. Which they were not. And the judge, well let's not say much about him except … let's say it was not a balanced trial. We should have seen this earlier and done more to keep the child soldiers in the forefront of the case."

"The judge's reaction?" I asked. "Did you expect it?"

She blurted an expletive. "Maybe, less because of the interview itself and more because of the prosecutor. The prosecutor refused to sign on to the limits the judge imposed on the Chamber."

"Legal limits?"

"No. The prosecutor knew his limits within the law. He was simply not interested in the formalities of deference and protocol the judge expected, he spoke out, he tested the waters, he wanted the reach of the trial to go beyond the Chamber, and this made the judge uncomfortable. The judge wanted to be in total control, and the prosecutor did not go along."

She was called away unexpectedly from her office for an urgent matter: "Stay, stay, stay," she said. "We'll talk."

She crossed the boundaries between roles with ease, she could be the diplomat when this was required, and with little effort she could strip away the stateswoman's veneer to advocate ardently for child rights – which she did often as we spoke. She also knew the law and the human rights literature, with enough experience in courtrooms to know the consequences of speaking out as she had done, and she knew as well what she was doing when she warned, as she did in the interview, that the trial had lost sight of the crimes, conscripting boys and girls in Lubanga's army and what happened to them once they were in.

When she returned she said, "Frankly, it was the prosecutor on trial as much as Lubanga."

"Did that soften the blow?" I asked. Did she feel that the judge's ill-disposition towards the prosecutor made his fierce reaction to her interview more palatable?

"There was no blow to soften. I was beyond feeling angry or ashamed since I – or rather we in the Office of the Prosecution – were beyond that at this stage in the trial. It was my fourth year in the office, and this was the only way to make known what was happening. There was no other way. We all agreed, and I now regret I did not say more. The prosecution team had been bullied by the judge, cowed and pushed into corners and interrupted with admonitions and asides and insistent demands. Fulford orchestrated the trial. Good judges do not do this. Trials have their pace and flow and do best when guided by a gentle hand, but Judge Fulford's was heavy. He interrupted and cajoled and coached the counsellors on how to conduct their questioning. The prosecution was always on the defensive. That is what the judge wanted, and we did not respond. The information was there but our team did not connect the dots. That is what I wanted to do, connect the dots, be honest about the intermediaries and who they really were and how much the Chamber misunderstood them."

It would not have been surprising if Béatrice Le Fraper du Helen had turned bitter about the fallout from the interview. She had been obliged to change jobs. She was held up to public ridicule. And yet she bore no ill-will, and I could not help but wonder as we exchanged good-byes how unlikely it was for a woman of such undeniable warmth to stick so sharply in the judge's craw.

chapter 14

Disorder in the Court

The debate about calling the intermediaries to the stand became ever more heated. Maître Mabille insisted it was essential to the integrity of the trial while the prosecution argued this betrayed their initial promises to maintain anonymity. The judge meanwhile scolded the prosecution for delaying the proceedings. Increasingly accusatory exchanges were leading to a "breakdown in relations."[1]

The disorder in the Court was obvious to everyone. It was obvious to the Court reporter for the *New York Times*, whose article in late 2010 was remarkably candid. The first case at the International Criminal Court, she wrote, "may be coming apart." She reported the lament of the lawyer monitoring the trial for the International Bar Association that the "substance of the case was lost in procedural tangles." She spoke about legal wrangling and secrecy. She quoted from her conversation with the normally even-handed William Schabas, a ranking scholar on the International Criminal Court, who was uncharacteristically blunt. "The whole trial has been a nightmare since the disputes between judges and the prosecutor began in 2008. Relations have become ugly and unhealthy. There appears almost a breakdown between the two sides."[2]

But it was not just the two sides. It was all three – the judge, the prosecutor, and Maître Mabille. The prosecutor refused to defer to the judge's demands in the Chamber. Judge Fulford heaped scorn on the prosecutor, while Maître Mabille jabbed relentlessly at his flank.

There would be no concessions on the intermediaries, the contentious matter of the moment.[3] Maître Mabille had been saying she would prove the intermediaries had told the witnesses to lie about their parents, about their schooling, and especially about being child soldiers, arguing that none of them had ever been child soldiers. The prosecution was persistent in their objections: intermediaries were not the type to conspire so systematically against the court or, for that matter, to make a false claim about a young man being a child soldier. After all, most of the intermediaries had worked in reintegration centres helping kids demobilize as they came to them for help. Why would they now use them in a way that would expose them to international shame?

On 12 May 2010, the judge ordered the prosecution's intermediaries to appear at The Hague. He then ordered the prosecutor to provide additional witnesses to explain to the Chamber how the intermediaries in Ituri had been contacted and how the intermediaries in turn had contacted the witnesses. Maître Mabille intended to scour the entire network of prosecution contacts in Ituri in hopes of finding something suspicious. It was sure to be an exasperating, time-consuming task, and the prosecution was not as convinced as the judge of the merit of gathering so many names. The judge meanwhile continued to address the prosecution with annoyance. Did the prosecution intend to complete the task as he had requested?

Ms Samson from the prosecution team explained to the judge the matter was still under discussion in her office. The judge's pique flared.

"The Chamber is extremely displeased as to the wholesale lack of activity in relation to this issue, which we expect to be rectified immediately."

It was not going to be rectified immediately, and once again the threat of suspension hung over the Chamber.

Two years before, in the lead up to the first stay, the prosecution had scrambled to find a solution: a summary of the information the defence team wanted, a list of potentially exculpatory facts, whatever was needed to appease the judge. This time was different. The prosecutor now knew the judge would end the trial without a conviction, even if it meant Mr Lubanga would be free to return to his political career in Bunia, and it mattered little what appeasing gestures the prosecution might make. The difference this time was that the prosecutor was ready to play hardball. He knew the judge's routine. He knew the judge would do anything to buttress his authority in the Chamber. This time the prosecutor stonewalled.

The Office of the Prosecution asked for more time to discuss matters within the team. The intermediaries as witnesses would need protection. Had the Court made the necessary arrangements? They would have to be kept safe in Ituri until they boarded the plane. Arrangements would have to be made in the courtroom to hide their identities and distort their voices. Where would they go once they were done? Had that been arranged? And what about those in danger who had no protection – the families of the witnesses or those who had collaborated with the prosecution?

But the judge was in a hurry and suspected the prosecution was stalling for time. By the first of June, two of the four intermediaries had been summoned to The Hague and they would soon testify; these two were under protection measures. The others were not, but the defence insisted on making a third intermediary known immediately without protection so they could raise questions about him with the first two. This brought matters to a head. On the fifth of July, the first intermediary was on the stand and the defence wanted to know what relations he had with the third, still unprotected intermediary. Mr Biju-Duval insisted the identity of the third intermediary be disclosed, and he did not want to wait the few days for protection measures to be arranged. He wanted to interrogate the third intermediary immediately.

The judge agreed, ordering that the identity of the third intermediary be disclosed within two hours.

The prosecution objected.

The judge was unfazed. He would ask the defence team kindly to keep his identity to themselves and that should suffice.

No, it would not suffice, replied the prosecution.

It is not clear why the judge refused to wait the few days for the protection measures or why he seemed willing to suspend the trial over so small a matter. When the prosecution objected, the judge became indignant. He listened with manufactured politeness and reiterated his order to disclose the third intermediary's identity instantly. The next day, the prosecution brought in another staff member, an expert on matters of protection, who urged the judge to consider the protection commitments he had previously made and the potential risk of naming the intermediary without the agreed-upon protection measures.

"The Court," the expert said, "does not have the discretion to leave a person unprotected if that were to serve other convenient interests of the Court. That's a fundamental absolute immutable duty."

The judge was smug. Of course he knew that. "On this point," he said to the expert with his trademark disdain, "on this point you're teaching your grandmother to suck eggs."

When the prosecution did not reveal the intermediary's identity, the judge summarily suspended the trial. He informed the Chamber that he had filed his decision with the registry to stay the proceedings and there would be no further filings, no further submissions, no further applications. The Court officer resident in the DR Congo would return to the Hague, and in a week, the judge would reconvene the Chamber to discuss the release of Mr Lubanga.

Is this it? I asked a friend at the court, an advisor to the prosecutor.

He smiled and hesitated.

Well ... perhaps it is, he replied. His trip the next day to Kinshasa had been cancelled. The long corridor of offices where counsellors and researchers had their offices had gone still.

What now? I asked. Could Lubanga go free?

Yes, of course.

And then?

What do you think?

Back to Ituri.

Where else?

And the UPC?

He is still the leader of the Hema. More than ever.

But now the Ugandans are gone, who will support him?

You've been there. You know the Hema, they are his supporters. Tschisekedi maybe, the political opposition. Diamond merchants from Lebanon. The Chinese.

Not possible.

Au contraire. He's a hero, victorious at the Court. He can do anything he wants. No one in Ituri, or anywhere in the DRC for that matter, knows what a stay is, and as far as anyone knows, Lubanga beat the Court. And you know how this plays in Ituri. Maji-maji. The guy turns bullets into water.

It's just a temporary halt to the trial, I added. No one won.

Lubanga won. The Hema are celebrating.

This is a disaster.

No, he said, it's a court case. It is also a disaster and it has been a disaster from the beginning.

So Lubanga goes back to Bunia.

Let's see. It will go to appeal.

Then what?

He smiled. He had already said enough. He held up a pencil and a piece of paper.

What's that? I asked.

He wrote something quickly on a Post-it note. He motioned for me to pass him my notebook. He opened it and stuck the Post-it on a random page.

He excused himself.

I leafed through the notebook and found the name, Gil Courtemanche.

I had heard of him. He had written a bestselling book a few years before with the title *Un dimanche à la piscine à Kigali*, about the love of a middle-aged filmmaker for a young Rwandan woman, and the tragedy that engulfed the two of them during the genocide. He had a reputation for weaving his personal life into his books and his books into his life so completely it was hard to tell where his writing and his passion for justice left off and his own life began. I would soon discover that he had taken a job – a real job, as he would later call it – at the International Criminal Court to chronicle the Lubanga trial, hired by the prosecutor himself. It was a natural enough progression; the Rwandan crisis of reciprocal ethnocide spilled over into the Congo, just as Gil Courtemanche's attention, ever wedded to real history, moved from the violence between ethnic enemies in the Rwandan crisis to something similar in Ituri. In 2005, the prosecutor offered him a job chronicling the Lubanga trial. He was given a space to work in the Office of the Prosecution with access to all the records and transcripts any writer could want.

He had a front row seat to the investigations in the lead up to the trial, a tale of atrocity and punishment in the unruly stretches of central Africa. Very promising material for a writer. Except he never figured on a trial Chamber so full of discord presided over by a judge who would declare the accused free before the trial had even begun. Dismayed by the serial failures of the Chamber, Gil Courtemanche quit his writing job at the Court after nearly three years and wrote the story as he feared it would unfold: the trial would abort and Lubanga would go free.

Le Monde, le lézard et moi[4] was published as a novel in 2009. The book's narrator works in the Office of the Prosecution, just as Gil Courtemanche had done, observing the trial career from one grinding halt to another with its singular cast of characters until, following a dispute over evidence, the judge stops the trial and declares Kabanga (a thinly disguised Lubanga) free to go. The Lubanga character, Kabanga, returns to a hero's welcome in Bunia. The narrator is deeply distressed at this turn of events, which he knows to be a miscarriage of justice, and leaves his job. He is adrift, miserable, and disturbed for a time, until he finally understands what he must do: travel to the town of Bunia in Ituri. He finds a room in a desultory hotel in Bunia among the mélange of displaced persons, prostitutes, refugees, and child soldiers going between home and warfare while Kabanga, holding court in the local bar, schemes to regain his power. As days go by, the narrator becomes obsessed with the outcome of the trial that has allowed Kabanga to parade about town freely, sowing the seeds of havoc. The narrator slips into his own heart of darkness, becoming more and more morose until his travelling companion leaves him and returns to The Hague. In the end, the narrator's only companion is a small green lizard.

It is a distressing rendering of the Lubanga trial. He had dared to write something nobody wanted to hear. I made contact with him, and we agreed to meet near his home in Montreal. I did not know at the time that he had become ill, and even the short walk to the neighbourhood café would be difficult for him.

I arrived in advance. Peering through the café's storefront window onto the street, I watched him approach at a hobble, holding on to a lamp post across the street and then shuffling his way through the snow, with the air of a man suffering from a terminal disease. He could not have been as old as he looked. He wore black from head to toe. He asked for a triple espresso.

Someone said of him once that he was not terribly comfortable with happiness. Nor was he likeable. I liked him at once. He did not smile, but I smiled when he spoke. He feigned a phenomenal disinterest, but he was phenomenally interesting. He cautioned me against believing everything I heard, but everything he said seemed credible. He was here against considerable odds, and it must have been for a reason.

We got down to business.

"Le livre, bien sûr." he said. "I've talked too much about that Lubanga book. It's an angry book and I had reason to be angry. Look at what's happening." It was early 2010, a few months before the second stay.

"The trial then."

"Well, it would have made anyone angry. Thomas Lubanga is a serious criminal and the trial was a sideshow, shouting from one side and another. The trial was not serious. It was not very serious when I was there and it got worse."

"Was this the book the prosecutor wanted you to write?"

"The prosecutor wanted a documentary of the trial. When I told him I was quitting to write a story about Lubanga's acquittal, I would not have blamed him if he had been angry, but he wasn't. He said, 'Excellent. Write it.' It bothered others but not him, not at all, because he knew why I wanted to write it and he did not mind people knowing what I would say about the turmoil in the Chamber. The prosecutor was a showman, some people did not like that, and he flouted courtroom manners and protocol, but make no mistake – he had integrity. It was easy to get the wrong impression because he was no saint. He could be obstinate. He had his weaknesses. He was too full of himself, marching here and there taking aim at bad guys, but believe it or not, he meant it, and he uses the law for what it was meant to be used. You could not say that about others in the trial."

"Did he ever tell you what he thought about the book?"

"Like I said, he thought the book might help."

"With the judge?"

"Well, that too. The judge had his favourites and the prosecutor was not one of them. Lubanga seemed to be the judge's favourite, strangely enough, since the Chamber had heard how Lubanga had commanded battalions of children, shot people in the anus, urged his men to exterminate villages, and still the judge favoured him, or so it seemed. The judge frankly did not seem terribly concerned about the outcome of the trial as much as whether it followed a few legal principles administered under his authority. He wanted the right kind of trial a lot more than the right kind of outcome."

Gil Courtemanche coughed and sputtered. For a moment I thought he might need medical attention. When he recovered, he managed a smile.

I asked him if there was something more I should know. About the trial.

He seemed on the verge of saying something and then he stopped himself.

"Non, ça suffira. That's enough."

Gil Courtemanche passed away a year and a half later on 19 August 2011.

~

The Chamber reconvened as planned, a week following the judge's decision to stay the trial.

As far as the judge was concerned, his decision was immutable. Any interventions from this point on that did not explicitly acknowledge the unassailable truths he had pronounced a week before were unacceptable. The door was closed.

The protection expert from the Office of the Prosecution did her best anyway. She argued that since the Chamber knew nothing about how the Appeals Chamber would rule on the matter, the judge's decision to release Lubanga could not be final. The judge might have strong opinions about the release of Thomas Lubanga, but it meant nothing without the Appeal Chamber's ruling.

The judge declared that his decision was unalterable and roundly dismissed the expert's intervention. He responded in the same obdurate manner to other objections to his decision, ignoring or dismissing them, and declaring once even more assertively that the prisoner should be released unconditionally.

There was one more piece of business. It was the judge's firm intention to punish the prosecutor – and here he no longer referred to the Office of the Prosecution but to Luis Moreno-Ocampo in person, along with the deputy prosecutor, Fatou Bensouda. Sanctions would be taken against both of them under Article 71 of the statute for "refusal to comply with the Chamber's orders" issued by the judge. This was an oral warning, which he assured would be implemented following the outcome of the appeal.

When the Appeals Chamber emerged from its deliberations three months later, its main concern was to wag a finger at the prosecutor for his disobedience. This seemed strangely beside the point, since the heart of the matter, the reason for the prosecution's reluctance to obey was the judge's order to expose the identities of witnesses before proper protection measures were in place. Only a few weeks before, Mercimungu had told the Court how he was threatened for agreeing to testify against Lubanga.

The Appeals Chamber gave only a glancing nod to the Chamber's nonchalance about protection. No mention was made of the judge's short-circuiting the protection process or his order to prematurely divulge the identities of the intermediaries in question. Protection measures could have been finalized within a short period, a few days in all likelihood, but the judge had shown no patience. He had given the order and expected immediate compliance from the prosecution.

To my reading, the ruling seemed oddly indifferent to the care the founders had taken to tune the Rome Statute to the complexities of protecting its helpers in the turbulent places where the Court would have jurisdiction. These are dangerous places. Testimonies are never just evidence, they are calculated risks. The statute took this under serious consideration, assigning some responsibilities to the Victims and Witnesses Unit inside the registrar, some to the prosecution, and some elsewhere, all covering different angles of protection. It might have seemed cumbersome to invest responsibility for protection in a confederacy of different organs described in a scattering of different articles. They might not all concur. But that was the point; it offered solid assurance against the possibility that a witness's fate would be sealed by one person and one person alone. Spreading responsibility around was deliberate, and a good idea.

The prosecution argued that protecting witnesses is a nuanced affair, with too much at stake for one presiding judge to rule with a monopoly over how best to keep safe those who risk their lives coming before a Chamber. This argument was deemed irrelevant: "There is no exception to the general principle that the Prosecutor (or other parties and participants) must follow the orders of the Trial Chamber when it comes to issues of protection." A bold statement and one seemingly at odds with the spirit of the statute. Was this the Appeals Chamber doing what it could to keep the unruly Chamber from fissuring further? It seemed more likely to have the opposite effect.

The decision was, in any event, a salvage operation. The trial would now have to be wrested from the dustbin. After buttressing the judge's authority in the Chamber and telling him he had every right to make the decision, the Appeals Chamber then let him know he had "erred" in taking the drastic remedy of suspending the trial when the problem was hardly more than the prosecution's reluctance to disclose information, not serious enough to render a fair trial impossible. Ending the trial at this midway point would have grave consequences.[5] It would leave the victims without any recourse – a grievous prospect for a Court that attended so proudly to the victims. It would have been a blow to the International Criminal Court and expectations for global justice, hardly something to neglect when the Court's credibility was at stake in Ituri and DR Congo and Africa and even farther afield.

The Appeals Chamber reversed Judge Fulford's decision to stay the trial. Lubanga would remain in detention. Witnesses waiting to testify who had returned to their homes or taken refuge while the Appeals Chamber deliberated would return to The Hague to wait their turn. No punishment would be meted out upon the prosecutor and his deputy, as the judge had presumptuously proposed. Testimony would resume in an already embattled Chamber.

chapter 15

Sexual Violence

It was common knowledge both inside and outside the Chamber that Lubanga's men had violated the young women and girls they recruited or captured. It was not just a matter of rape, because rape in the Democratic Republic of the Congo during these years covered a full arsenal of sexual violence. The common denominator was armed men forcing themselves on young women, but these men also penetrated girls with various objects, or they raped them aggressively in front of family members to show their prowess. Or they kept them as slaves for months often impregnating them and sending them away to the poor towns in the hinterlands of Ituri, where they had to establish some sort of life away from their families who had shunned them.

Sexual violence was everywhere, and hardly anyone could speak honestly about child soldiers or the events in Ituri without telling stories of what had happened to young girls. The fate of boys was as expected: they were taught to shoot and they were marched into battle. The girls, on the other hand, were taken and trained and then frequently became concubines for commanders or their men. The spectre of sexual violence lurked underneath nearly all of the testimonies heard over the course of the trial. There was the case of the commander in Mahagi who kept a harem of girls for his pleasure. There was the boy recruit in one of the camps who had the job of finding girls for each of the commanders and then taking them away when he was done. There were girls who became pregnant, were left on their own and forced into prostitution. One woman, it was said, whose son had been seized as a recruit, begged the boy's commander to let him go. In return, she was raped on the spot, in front of her son.

Sexual violence was an inextricable part of war in Ituri, and yet it was rarely a welcome topic in the trial. It came up, of course, but it was readily dismissed. On occasion it sprang up unexpectedly as part of another topic, but no one ever doubted the judge would look for a way to limit the discussion. Only when the associate judge from Costa Rica, Elizabeth Odio Benito, insisted on asking witnesses about girl soldiers did the judge relent and allow it, but this was rare, for he had little time for what he felt were diversions from the courtroom's main considerations. This business of sexual violence was a diversion that could pull the trial into a time-consuming morass.

The Democratic Republic of the Congo is known as the rape capital of the world, and for good reason. The overthrow of Joseph Mobutu Sese Seko in the mid-nineties left bare a state that had never much functioned anyway and now functioned almost not at all. If there had been any public services to speak of under Mobutu, after his fall there were none. If there were customs posts before, now there were only border posts making private deals with passing vehicles. If there had been police in the past, now there were vigilantes. Those who had lived under Mobutu, rapacious that he was, spoke of even more moral decay in the post-Mobutu era as the state frittered into nothing and in its place criminals and rebel groups sprang up as government personnel. Some of them were supported by Rwanda or Uganda or Zimbabwe, and some were supported by rising political figures in the Congo, all dealing gems and metals or timber for guns, and all preying on civilians. It was a new era, an era without church or state or inhibition, ruled by the random spread of weapons and the wanton use of force, and with nothing to stop them, the armed men had their furious way with women.

By the time Lubanga returned to Ituri in 2002, sexual violence was rampant. Rape and conflict went together as a matter of course; rebel gangs invaded communities and villages and seized women, as if women, young and old, were war's booty and sexual violence a conventional weapon.[1] This was nothing new, and the world had already witnessed such things in the conflicts of Kosovo, Rwanda, Sierra Leone, and Liberia. But the DR Congo was different from these places in its brutality and the sheer numbers of women who were abused. Cases ran into the thousands. Rapists could do as they wished with impunity. The Tribunal of First Instance in Bunia was closed because of insecurity in the region and the judges were intimidated, leaving the rapists to conclude it was their right to slake their desires in the unlawful fashion that had become the norm. The only thing to do was give the young women medical treatment after the fact and solace for their wounds. The Panzi Clinic founded by the heroic Dr Denis Mukegwe opened in Bukavu in 1999 originally as a gynaecological service and in ten years treated more than ten thousand raped and abused women. Foundation Rama Levina clinic in South Kivu treated more than seven hundred victims in the course of a year beginning in mid-2010. Médecins sans frontière opened the Baraka Clinic near Shabunda in 2004, which received over five hundred women in the first six months. Another clinic in Ituri treated nearly three thousand rape victims between 2010 and 2011.

Some clinics were supported by money from non-government organizations, while others received funds from United Nations agencies and overseas benefactors. Lubanga's trial took place in the shadow of these dozens of centres, where the legacy of women's injuries was testimony itself and it was difficult if not anomalous to ignore, especially since Lubanga and his commanders were as guilty as anyone. Everyone knew what they had done and not because it was something widely talked about but because the acts were so commonplace it was impossible not to know about them. The victims could be found waiting in lines at the makeshift clinics with foreign doctors. There were human rights advocates at the time who were as eager to hear what happened to them as the victims were to tell it. Whenever the fighting increased, as it did in May 2003 amidst rumours that an international force might soon be arriving, instances of rapes spiked dramatically. Brigitte, a slight girl of fifteen, gave an account to a Human Rights Watch researcher:

I was sent by my family to get an axe in town. When I was coming back
I met a group of UPC [Lubanga's army] combatants in Mudzipela near

the Radio Candip station. One of them took me by force into a nearby house. The people who were in the house ran out as soon as they saw him. He tore my clothes off and then he raped me. It was my first time. He told me he would shoot me if I shouted. I went home and told my mother. She took me with her to the military camp and I recognized the man who had raped me, but he fled. The officer told my mother he would give her some money to take me to hospital but he never did.[2]

The perpetrator was never brought to trial.

Only a few witnesses spoke directly about sexual abuse during the trial. One was a young man we will call Jambo Muzuri. He testified as a child soldier witness before the Chamber in mid-March 2009 at the early stages of the trial. There was nothing remarkable about this young man. He was eighteen or nineteen years old at the time of the trial, a fellow of slight build with a modest demeanour. He had fallen in by default with Governor Molondo Lompondo's ragtag army in 2000, and when Governor Molondo Lompondo was run out of town in August 2002, Jambo Muzuri, a Hema, slipped over to the other side and joined Lubanga's army. He was ten or eleven years old at the time.

He had not been abducted or incarcerated in a military camp. He had not been coerced by family members. There were no double identities or dramatic escapes and recaptures with beatings by Lubanga's officers. He was just a boy who had been on his way home from school when he heard fighting coming from his neighbourhood and, arriving there, he discovered the entire neighbourhood had disappeared or been forced to flee. His family was among them and he did not know where they had gone. The safest thing was to make his way to the house of a family friend, a soldier. The man took him in, gave him something to eat and a place to stay, and there in the compound of this army man he lived under the pretence of being a soldier until he was one. It made little difference whether he was fighting against the Hema or with them, whether he was a bodyguard in the governor's camp outside of

Bunia or at the UPC camp at Mandro. He had lost his parents and he had little choice but to seek refuge wherever he could.

As a witness, he recounted, in the way a grocer might review his inventory, the things that happened to him and the things he saw as if they just simply occurred, as if events like these were too common to merit embellishing. He responded to the two days of questioning without guile. When the prosecution asked him if he had done any special services as a bodyguard for his first commander, he gave his deadpan account.

"He asked me to go and arrest people."

"Why?"

"If he asked me to go and arrest people, I would do it. Maybe they were carrying weapons without the commander's permission or maybe they had escaped. Maybe they owed him money."

"Anything else?"

"If the commander wanted a girl, he sent me out to get one."

"Do you know what the commander did with the girls you got for him?"

"They went to his bedroom."

"How old were the girls?"

"Some were adults and some were maybe fifteen, too young. I was asked to go and get a young girl one time. She was young and in the second form in secondary school. I didn't do it. The commander was furious."

"Did the girls want to go or did you have to force them?"

"Some were forced."

"Do you know what happened if the girls would resist?"

"They couldn't."

"So this was for your own commander, but what about other commanders? Did they do the same?"

"Same with the others."

The testimony of Jambo Muzuri begged the question of whether justice would rightly be served if the trial considered nothing other than the single charge of recruiting child soldiers, a charge that was self-evident. More to the point and particular to the Lubanga case was whether kidnapping and forcing girls into the bedrooms of commanders and more generally into sexual slavery was a war crime. And if so, was it the obligation of the Chamber in the Lubanga case to include sexual violence in the charges?

The associate judge, Elizabeth Odio Benito, phrased the question in a particularly nuanced way: if it was a crime when Lubanga's men raped or killed their enemies, was it any less so if they did the same to young girls recruited as child soldiers under their own command?

~

That was a burning question no one wanted to touch, for if it were taken seriously it meant the original charge would have to be changed. None of the main actors in the Chamber wanted that, for reasons of their own.

Among several elephants in the room, sexual violence was the largest. NGOs and journalists, legal activists, UN officers, and celebrities all watching the trial felt strongly something had to be done. But it was difficult for evidence about sexual violence to penetrate the judge's wall of indifference, even for the expert witness Christine Peduto, who had personally overseen the demobilization of young women soldiers in Bunia.

Christine Peduto had kept records on sexual violence and would speak about the matter when asked. She had been present during Lubanga's worst rampages, when his men razed settlements and seized local girls for their pleasure. All of this appeared in the affidavit she provided in advance of her testimony. Still, no one asked, neither the interrogator for the prosecution nor the interrogator for the defence. It had been only towards the end of her interrogation that Mr Diakiase, a counsellor for a group of victims, stepped forward and broke the silence, asking her what in fact had befallen the young women.

Christine Peduto replied, "Yes, there had been quite a few young girls from Lubanga's UPC army in the demobilization centres, and all of them had been sexually abused by their commanders and sometimes by other soldiers. The girls had to spend the night in a separate area of the camp, but everyone knew that some of them were taken to spend the night with the officers. We knew what happened to these young girls. It was catastrophic. I am talking about the physical and psychological effects. Some had become pregnant and some had abortions, voluntary or involuntary, and some of these abortions were done in terrible conditions."

The judge decided this was the moment for a break.

When proceedings resumed, Mr Diakiase once again tried to raise the question. There were frequent interruptions. The judge had some administrative matters. Maître Mabille's associate requested the Chamber to have Ms Peduto hand over the notes she was making or had made during the examination. There was a debate.

Would she elaborate on the physical state of the girls? asked Mr Diakiase.

"I have in mind the situation of one of these young girls," she said, "who had several abortions and who had to be referred to the emergency unit of the hospital in Bunia for care, and she spent a lot of time in hospital before she could recover. She was like others who became pregnant, sometimes many times, after spending several months or even years in armed groups without receiving appropriate care, the type of care you give to a pregnant woman. So they needed attention with respect to their health and their food and all this. They had nowhere to go. They were thrown out by the commanders when they were no longer needed for sexual pleasure, and it meant out of the commander's group. They could go into demobilization centres if they wanted, but they could not go home. Many went back to the armed groups of the commanders who had used them."

There had been polite nods in the Chamber.

When another expert witness, Radhika Coomaraswamy, made an appearance some months later, she was less retiring, more forthright than Christine Peduto had been, and more difficult to dismiss. She was the secretary general's special envoy on children in armed combat, self-possessed and unapologetic. She seemed impervious to the judge's politely officious demeanour. Nor was she particularly perturbed when the judge informed her that the Chamber had met prior to her appearance and agreed there were issues not to be raised during her examination. The Chamber, the judge advised her, would be pleased to benefit from her broad professional experience and hear general information from her on child soldiers. As far as the particulars of the DRC were concerned, that was better left to the local expert. As an example, she should not hesitate to help the Court understand how she understood the phrase "participate actively in hostilities" when it came to young girls generally, but the particulars of their experience in Ituri or their treatment in camps or the fallout from their experience were not items of interest to the Court.

Ms Coomaraswamy nodded politely. She sat comfortably at the witness table, and after responding to a few questions about her broad views on child soldiers, there was finally the question of young girls. She answered as if she had heard nothing of the judge's embargo, speaking frankly about the criminal abuse of girl soldiers in the Democratic Republic of the Congo and Ituri and Bunia. It did not matter, she said, whether they participated in hostilities or whether they brought food or gave commanders pleasure; these were all crimes under the statute. Making any child a soldier was a crime, whether it occurred in the Congo or elsewhere. Children are too young to understand the dangers of war and the particulars of death, even if they come into the armed forces of their own accord. They are there onfalse pretenses. Abuse of female soldiers simply magnifies the crime, and it matters little whether they are subject to sexual abuse or whether they cook for a commander or take messages or kill for a commander; they are still victims of criminal acts. If they are raped, they become victims twice-fold.

She spoke with the assurance of someone explaining the Charter of Human Rights to a first-year class on humanitarian law.

"Your Honour," she said, "it is important that your rulings protect all affected children and do not ignore the central abuse perpetrated against girls during their association with armed groups after they have been recruited or enlisted, regardless of whether or not they engaged in direct combat functions during conflict. It is important to give these girls justice for the whole panoply of abuse suffered when they were taken and used by armed groups, girls whose futures at the age of twelve, thirteen, and fourteen years of age are sadly warped by their horrible experiences."

The defence objected. Ms Coomaraswamy had gone beyond the guidelines on which the Chamber had agreed, and this was not acceptable. Her testimony should be struck from the record. The judge hesitated before sustaining the objection. He could not now turn back the testimony, nor did he wish to stand in the way of this wilful woman who without apologies had handily stepped outside the boundaries he had taken pains to draw. He paused in a rare moment of indecision. He would, he promised the Chamber, review the witness's testimony for relevance to the expectations of the Chamber, and only the portions meeting the Chamber's relevance criteria would be accepted into evidence.

Day by day, discussions about sexual violence surfaced, sometimes out of the blue and sometimes calculated, in spite of the Chamber's efforts to keep them away. The eminent Chilean human rights investigator Robert Garreton presented his brief on human rights violations in the Congo and spoke lengthily about sexual abuse,[3] though, in the end, his report, like the reports of other expert witnesses, was received politely and shelved. The Chamber seemed only faintly interested. The victims with their representatives had earlier risen up against the judge and against his ban on discussing sexual violence and had reminded the Chamber that the purpose of the law was not only to protect the accused or the legal prerogatives of the defence or to keep the prosecutor in his place but to protect those who, like themselves, had been victimized by warlords like Mr Lubanga. Their petition had been denied, despite the fact that a quarter of the recognized victims had been sexually abused, and the majority were girls.

Only one person in the trial Chamber dared to defy Judge Fulford's ban on the subject of sexual violence against girls, and that was the associate judge, Elizabeth Odio Benito. She did not speak out often, but when the subject came up, she would boldly put forward a question about girl recruits and what had happened to them. Judge Fulford had little choice but to cede her the floor.

Elizabeth Odio Benito was born in the hardscrabble Costa Rican port town of Puntarenas into a family of judges and politicians, and there she grew up in two separate worlds. One was the world of her father, the member of Parliament, and her grandfather the judge, and another was the world of this derelict port city on the Pacific coast, a world of hard-bitten families and women struggling to sustain them. She was a woman in a man's world. In school she was at the head of a class of boys, she wanted to play football but was not allowed, and she could swim but was advised she shouldn't. She knew from an early age that she was destined to connect the two worlds of her youth, to place the skills of her fathers in the service of poor women. She knew this would not be easy.

She excelled in law and her reputation grew steadily after graduation. She represented Costa Rica at human rights conferences, served on international law commissions, served twice as Costa Rica's minister of justice, and then as Costa Rica's second vice-president. In 1993, her career path took a sharp turn when the UN General Assembly selected her to serve as a judge at the International Criminal Tribunal for the former Yugoslavia, and there she urged the Chamber to have a fresh look at sexual slavery, forced prostitution, and other forms of sexual violence that came shockingly to the fore. Sexual violence was not then a separate crime, something that was about to change.

When the newly formed International Criminal Court selected Ms Benito among the first cohort of judges, it was an obvious choice. But like other steps in her career, it did not come easily. Shortly after her nomination, Costa Rica's president blocked her confirmation. He never said why, though it was clear he did not want his name paired with a woman who stood for women's rights and access to abortions in Costa Rica, this in spite of the fact that she had served two distinguished terms as minister of justice under previous regimes. His decision caused a scandal, and it was not long before a group of prominent women jurists from Latin America protested the president's refusal to confirm her nomination. One member of this group, the president of Panama, put Elizabeth Odio Benito's name forward as the choice of her own country. Never before had a judge been nominated by a country other than her own.

By the time of the Lubanga trial, sexual violence had made its way into the Rome Statute among the corpus of war crimes and crimes against humanity. Rape and sexual slavery were by now formal crimes and by all rights should have been included in the charges against Lubanga. The Court had all of the legal armour it needed, other than a willing judge. When the victims asked that rape and sexual slavery be added to the charges, Judge Benito joined the other associate judge in writing the majority decision in support of the idea. Judge Fulford remained resolutely opposed.

Judge Benito had still more to say on the matter. Rather than simply accept the judge's decision, she wrote a brief explaining why it was wrong. The decision was wrong because it failed to recognize that sexual violence was inseparable from the charge of recruiting, conscripting, and using children in war. Indeed, it could just as well be seen as an "aggravating element," a seriously aggravating element, to be sure, though not a separate crime altogether.[4]

The problem as she saw it was that the judge, for reasons of his own, was loath to allow sexual abuse as a part of the case, whether as a formal charge or as an aggravating element. He might have been worried this heated claim with its lengthy polemics and sexual content would draw out the trial even longer. Her point was there was no need to amend the charge. She argued that exposing children to the dangers of battle was hardly any different from exposing them to the dangers of sexual aggression; both were harmful and both stemmed directly from the act of recruitment. It made no sense to charge Lubanga with exposing children to danger by asking them to inflict violence on others while turning a blind eye to exposing children to the danger that their own commanders deliberately and intentionally inflicted on them. The only difference was that in one case it was the enemy who brought harm to the children and in the other it was Lubanga's own rank and file. In her words,

Children are protected from child recruitment not only because they can be at risk for being a potential target to the "enemy" but also because they will be at risk from their "own" armed group who has recruited them and will subject these children to brutal trainings, torture and ill-treatment, sexual violence and other activities and living conditions that are incompatible and in violation to these children's fundamental rights. The risk for children who are enlisted, conscripted or used by an armed group inevitably also comes from within the same armed group.[5]

It was certainly a crime to send innocent children firing wildly into enemy lines not knowing fully why they were doing it. They could get hurt or killed. They did get hurt. But from a legal perspective, she asked, was it any different when their own commanders raped or abused or injured them?

~

As the trial drew to a close, the judge became even more adamant about keeping the subject of rape and violence against women out of the courtroom. Nothing was said for fear of the judge's scorn, except for one final, conclusive moment.

The prosecution counsellor Ms Samson had taken the floor during the closing arguments. She referred briefly to the testimony of none other than Jambo Muzuri, one among a dozen key moments she recalled to summarize the case. She reminded the Chamber how he was used as a child soldier to guard the compound of his commander and run errands, and how he had fetched girls for the commander to do with as he wished. She reminded the Chamber that Jambo Muzuri was a typical child soldier, he did not much like his commander but he obeyed him because he had no choice. He was a child. He was used actively in hostilities, and among his hostile acts was to bring young women to the commander.

Ms Sampson's summary was no more remarkable than anything else in the morning of summaries, but her reference to Jambo Muzuri pricked the judge's composure. Had they not agreed, he wanted to know, that there was a line to be drawn between using child soldiers on the battlefield and using child soldiers for other tasks such as cooking or running errands or getting girls for the commanders to sleep with?

"Now, I want there to be no confusion about this," the judge said. "You are saying – is this right? – that if an individual is sent out to select women, young women, for commanders to sleep

with, that falls on the side of the dividing line of participating actively in hostilities."

Ms Samson knew it was a loaded question. She hesitated. It was
then the prosecutor boldly jumped in.

"Say yes," said the Prosecutor without rising or asking for the
floor. This stoked the judge's temper further.

"If I may," asked the prosecutor seeking the floor.

"Please, Mr Ocampo," said the judge. "I am speaking with
Ms Samson."

"Are you saying," said the judge, turning to Ms Samson, "that
selecting young women is participating in hostilities?"

"That's correct."

Once again, the prosecutor asked to be recognized. "If I may ..."

"Mr Ocampo, really, can we please have some order as to how
the submissions are advanced? I am not going to have different
people jumping up and intervening."

This was the last the Chamber would hear about sexual violence.

chapter 16

A Dubious Conviction

As the Lubanga trial staggered to a close, Maître Mabille seemed likely to come out the winner. No one knew for sure, but she was the odds-on favourite, even though the evidence of Lubanga's guilt could not have been more palpable, since there were videos and reports and verbal testimonies all making clear there were not just a few child soldiers conscripted into Lubanga's forces but whole platoons of them. The problem was there were considerations and issues in play that had little to do with the evidence. Maître Mabille hammered home her contention that the child soldiers interviewed were giving false information to the Court and that there was a conspiracy by the Prosecution's Office to keep these falsehoods from being known. There was no one to challenge her, much less the judge. The outcome hung in a precarious balance, and even those who were in a position to know only shrugged their shoulders when the question of the verdict arose.

Moreno-Ocampo might well have suspected the judge was leaning in this direction, and to ward off a disaster he arranged for the closing arguments to be a political gala. Celebrities would be in attendance. Angelina Jolie would be there. Humanitarian NGOs from around the world would be there, along with UN special envoys and prominent advocates of children's rights. The press would be there in full force: interviews, rehearsals, and side meetings, and then the closing arguments. The prosecutor turned what otherwise might have been a trial's last lugubrious days into an international gathering of concerned citizens in an effort to ensure that if the judge were to eventually let Lubanga go, the world would be watching.

For the first time since the beginning of the trial, the public gallery was full. Visitors were asked to show their credentials at the door. There was the full complement of counsellors from the prosecution and the defence. The judge was at his most decorous, graciously cajoling at times, beneficent or tactfully admonishing when need be. Lubanga was dressed in a dark blue suit, a baby blue shirt with a red and black silk square in the pocket puff to match the tie. On the first of two days, three members of the prosecution summarized aspects of the case until, at the close of the day, the judge recognized a frail gentleman advanced in age who stood with the help of an aide. When he spoke, a hush fell over the chamber and the gallery.

"Mr Ferencz," said the judge.

Ben Ferencz is the only jurist still living from among the prosecutors at the Nuremberg trials. That was sixty-five years ago, and in those years he had guided the cause of international law and the institutions that led to the formation of this very Court.

He spoke eloquently of the events that led him at an early age to prosecute first the Germans who had committed crimes against American troops, and then the special military units, the *Einsatzgruppen*, that followed on the heels of Hitler's invasions into Poland and the Soviet Union eliminating Jews, Gypsies, and a host of others. When the United States entered the Second World War, Ben Ferencz had applied to serve in army intelligence, but his Romanian birth disqualified him. He was too short for the Air Force anyway, and with no other alternative he ended up a private in General Patton's Third Army pursuing Germans across the Rhine. When it was discovered towards the end of the war that he had graduated from Harvard Law, he was transferred to an office still in Patton's Third Army, dealing with war crimes, and this new assignment led him into a gruesome life-changing experience. He was among the first of the Allied soldiers to enter the camps at Buchenwald and Mauthausen, where he memorably saw strewn about the grounds "putrid bodies of the dead and dying," and these images of horror changed the course of his life. He did his job collecting camp records, affidavits of torture and mass graves; he smelled the stench of burned bodies and witnessed the emaciation of the survivors. It was traumatic and "that trauma," he said in his brief, "was indelible and will remain with me forever."

It was a moving testimony.

"May it please your Honours," he said. "This is an historic moment in the evolution of international criminal law. For the first time, a permanent international court hears the closing statement for the prosecution as it concludes its first case against its first accused, Mr Thomas Lubanga Dyilo.

"I participated in this evolution. I have spent a lifetime striving for a more humane world governed by the rule of law. I am honoured to represent the prosecutor and to share some personal observations regarding the significance of the trial.

"Now in this trial, the evidence showed that waves of children recruited under Mr Lubanga's command moved through as many as twenty training camps, some holding between 8 and 1,600 children under age fifteen. But words and figures cannot adequately portray the physical and psychological harm inflicted on vulnerable children who were brutalized and who lived in constant fear. The loss and grief to the inconsolable families is immeasurable. Their childhood stolen, deprived of education and all human rights, the suffering of the young victims and their families left permanent scars. We must try to restore the faith of children so that they may join in restoring the shattered world from which they came."

After a brief pause, Mr Ferencz went on.

"All of these events, which the prosecution has carefully presented, have been proved beyond reasonable doubt.

"Let the voice and the verdict of this esteemed global court now speak for the awakened conscience of the world."

The first day of the closing arguments came to a close on the buoyant hope that the historical weight of Ben Ferencz's presence would lessen the likelihood of an acquittal.

As a mischievous youngster I had a yen for inventing stories. If someone asked what had happened on the way home from school,

I made up an encounter with gangsters, with little thought to whether or not I'd be believed. Maître Mabille, on the other hand, did expect to be believed; she instructed the Court in all candour that the prosecution had not only done a poor job of investigating but to cover its failings had conspired to have its witnesses – child soldiers and their go-betweens – concoct stories of how they had been abducted by force and treated abysmally to make their case credible. Here was her proof: the prosecution obstructed the truth. Maître Mabille's delivery soared with the assurance of a locomotive as she proclaimed once again that every one of the nine key child soldier witnesses lied to the Chamber under instructions from the prosecution.

"We know that to be a fact."

"And why did they lie?" Simple, she said. When the big boss of the International Criminal Court came before traumatized Congolese youngsters and offered money and a chance to get out of their village or even the DR Congo under a protection scheme, they agreed. It was no mystery, she said, they were paid to lie.

The prosecution's scheme, she explained, was carefully orchestrated to conceal a tissue of deceptions. It was, she pronounced confidently, a conspiracy. The prosecution – and here her trademark admonishing tone wagged volubly – arranged for those in contact with the witnesses to guide the spin they wanted on their testimony carefully while the prosecution promised to protect the go-betweens under a "seal of anonymity." That way, she announced to the Court, the prosecution thought no one would ever know as one witness after another gave the version of events they were coached to give – they were paid to give – by the intermediaries who had had contact with the witnesses under clear instructions. But they did.

As the second day of closing arguments drifted into the afternoon, Maître Mabille reminded the Court that Thomas Lubanga himself had issued decrees prohibiting the conscription of minors. He had brought them no harm; he was their protector. Of course those who had closely followed the events knew she was not telling the full story. Lubanga's first decree was issued shortly after a United Nations delegation had warned him that using child soldiers was a serious crime and the world was watching. Lubanga had done nothing except issue a decree. Maître Mabille wanted the Court to believe he had acted on his own volition.

I rose as the session came to a close to return to my small B&B some distance away, walked a little, took the bus for a few blocks and a trolley to the outskirts of Delft, where I had found an affordable room, a place to reflect. Maître Mabille had complained in Court about so many lies, how they were everywhere beclouding anything conclusive the prosecution might adduce or any shred of evidence that might be salvaged from their inept investigations. The one fact for her unspoiled by lies was that Thomas Lubanga, contrary to all the falsehoods, was a man of good intentions with the best interests of his people at heart. He was the saviour of Ituri, not the butcher the liars would have us believe he was. As the day came to a close, with her pronouncements still echoing in the Chamber, it seemed fearsomely possible she might carry the day.

~

It would be another seven months before the Chamber convened again. On 13 March 2012 the judges submitted their decision in a detailed 600-page chronicle of the trial with the simple conclusion that Lubanga was guilty of recruiting, conscripting, and using under-age children in hostilities. That was welcome, if unexpected.

It was far from clear at the time what this meant, since it would take yet another four months before the Chamber would reconvene for the sentencing. The question was whether the judge regarded Lubanga's responsibility to be light or severe, and whether his years in prison should be the maximum or the minimum or something in between. It made a difference. A maximum penalty would take a strong stand against impunity. It would have an impact on the commanders, the warlords, and perhaps even some presidents-for-life on what might feasibly be in store for them. A minimal sentence would do the reverse, declare that crimes of this nature could be committed with modest consequences. As it turned out, the sentence given to Lubanga was minimal. The prosecution had recommended the maximum twenty-eight years in prison, arguing that the accused had clearly committed the crimes and had committed them in multiples, unapologetically and in full knowledge of the offence he was committing. The judge disagreed. He cut the years proposed by the prosecution in half and subtracted from them the years Lubanga had already served, which would allow Lubanga, with an early pardon, to return to Ituri in a few short years.

Thomas Lubanga was not the only guilty party named in the judges' sentencing brief. The Office of the Prosecution received nearly as much guilty mention as Lubanga did. The prosecutor himself was declared guilty of not conducting a proper investigation and especially culpable for not checking the reliability of his witnesses. He had failed to verify the truth of his witnesses' testimonies, and the judge resented it. He resented the time needed to inquire into the relationship between the intermediaries and the witnesses, what in fact the intermediaries really asked of the witnesses, and just how much the intermediaries had coached the witnesses. *Deprecate* is a word that is not heard very often because it is harsh and belittling but *deprecate* was the word the judge used in chastising the prosecutor for his approach to the issue of sexual violence. The judge deprecated the prosecutor for choosing not to include sexual violence in the charges at first and then later for suggesting it ought to be considered as an aggravating factor.

The animus the judge harboured towards the prosecutor was jarring, particularly when Lubanga fared somewhat better. The judge took pains to note that Mr Lubanga had comported himself quite respectfully during the trial, in spite of the "onerous circumstances" for which the prosecutor himself was largely responsible. He made a point of reminding the Chamber that Lubanga had remained cooperative, even when the prosecutor stooped so low as to allow one of his staff to speak to the press about the trial. He appreciated Lubanga's patience in the face of the prosecutor's persistent aggravations, and as far as he was concerned, these good manners in the face of such aggravations counted as mitigating factors when it came to the sentencing. All things considered, Mr Lubanga came out rather well.

Few of those I knew to be following the trial had much to say. They were none too pleased, but they were also quietly thankful since they knew it could have been worse; the judge could have acquitted Lubanga and sent him happily home to Bunia. It was difficult to make much sense of it. In fact, it was impossible to fathom how the mitigating circumstances the judge took pains to elaborate had anything to do with what had happened in Ituri or the crimes themselves, or why these circumstances should be mitigating anyway. The courtroom theatrics that had spun out of the ongoing battle in the Chamber perversely assumed more importance than what the Chamber had heard about Ituri in 2002. Somewhere along the line, things had taken a strange turn: the crimes had themselves faded away from the main stage, leaving the legal theatrics front and centre.

How could this happen? It was hardly befitting this new Court that was supposed to be above the rattle and hum of lesser courts, which everyone knew were easily disrupted by courtroom gamesmanship. This Court with its international mandate and the treaty commitment of most of the world states was not supposed to allow raucous legal theatrics. Yet this is exactly what characterized the trial from the beginning. The Chamber and the roles of the players, even the pomp of the costumes and the roles in the Chamber were modelled on a dramatis personae that was only too familiar: there was the presiding judge with considerable powers, adversarial attorneys vying for victory and attention, bailiffs and the clerks and other minions arrayed in a manner that bespoke the Court's domestic common law court lineage. The main actors in the Chamber not only played these roles but played them with unusual fervour, probably with more fervour than the founders could have ever anticipated.

It was especially anomalous because adjudicating war crimes in international courts differs patently from adjudicating domestic criminal acts. Crimes that come before domestic courts are smaller. Most murders and thefts, fraudulent acts and sexual abuse are the work of one or two individuals and they do not take very long to commit. They are single events in a brief period of time, impulsive for the most part and, except in odd cases, clandestine.

Domestic courts adjudicating manslaughter cases have a lot of work to do in discovery. In coming to a decision on manslaughter cases domestic courts have to worry about whether they have the details right: have they got the right person, the right time, an accurate picture of the defendant's intentions? Courts must have a reasonable way to put evidence to the test and they do so, for all to see, by pitting one view against another. The assumption is that if competing versions of the truth come together in a lawyer's contest, the chaff will fall away, and once the dust settles, the truth of the case will become clear. Adversarial actors help in these cases, since the contest between opposing sides teases out the truth more assuredly than if there were only one judicial authority. It helps get to the real bottom of things. But is this really necessary in international courts?

In only the rarest circumstances, after all, does someone come forward in domestic cases of manslaughter or sexual abuse who happened to have seen the whole thing. It is even more rare for a lot of people to come forward who happened to have been there, saw what was happening, and proceeded to write extended reports on what they witnessed, including names, dates, and details. But this is commonly what happens in international criminal cases.

In this and other ways, the common law tradition, which largely governs the Court's procedures, seemed an awkward fit when adjudicating the Lubanga case. Lubanga's crimes were not isolated affairs. When he set about attacking neighbouring communities of different tribes, the Lendu and the Bira and others, there was nothing clandestine about it. Lubanga was proud of his atrocities against his tribal enemies. He was proud of the loyalty of his tribal kin who were willing to give up their small children for his cause, and he flaunted his success as a warlord with despotic intentions. He flaunted his campaign to eliminate those working in the goldfields so he could use the gold to buy arms. All this took place on a large scale, and he made little effort to hide what he was doing from the legions of NGO observers or UN human rights reporters or journalists on site to chronicle events for a news media with a hunger for war and conflict zones. The discovery process for war crimes in conflict zones is special because, unlike most crimes before domestic courts, there is always someone watching and there is a lot to write about. In the Lubanga case, child soldiers were everywhere. It was not as if there were only a few that UN Child Protection staff had to ferret out or social workers had to find among hundreds of soldiers.

In the face of overwhelming evidence, Maître Mabille did what ambitious defence lawyers do in lesser courts where the common law tradition sanctions an adversarial contest between two sides of the Chamber. She made exorbitant claims no one could disprove. It was her prerogative. She asserted unequivocally that Lubanga had nothing to do with the crimes whatsoever. It was quixotic, given what was known and what was easily knowable. She dared legal commentators to challenge her audacity and, of course, no one did. Nor did anyone ever challenge the licence the judge gave her to do it.

The adversarial encounters between the defence and the prosecution ought by rights and by the norms of common law trials to winnow out the truth from the chaff of the case. This did not happen in the Lubanga trial.[1] The course of the trial was never stable. It tottered on the brink of either collapse or discord on a number of occasions, unsure of its direction, buffeted in one direction or another by the judge, a prosecution that wanted to steer clear of the judge's objections and the excessive but persistent claims of Maître Mabille, but could not. Maître Mabille knew this, and she also knew that in the midst of this uncertainty she could bring the Chamber to a standstill, very much to her advantage. Other judges might have been able to more adroitly find a middle ground, but not Judge Fulford. The inevitable discord took over, leaving the space for constructive dialogue so small that, towards the end of the trial, the judge presided over very little more than a grumbling hive. The judge's final decision was as much an exit strategy as a verdict.

In the second year of the trial, I happened to be in Bunia on an assignment with the United Nations to examine what the UN agencies were doing in the area to promote peace. The United Nations was funding a number of disarmament projects. There were cash vouchers and job-training programs for those who were willing to surrender their weapons. Everywhere there was support for village committees monitoring the peace, where the women in charge took their responsibilities as custodians of the peace seriously; they dealt harshly with the slightest hint of conflict, and it was working. Health clinics where one or another ethnic group had previously felt unwelcome served twice as many clients now that open doors to all was a condition of funding. These projects were doing well; most Iturians desperately wanted peace.

On one occasion, I took a three-day trip north towards a stronghold of Lubanga's Hema supporters in the town of Fataki. The town was a string of shops along a yellow-brown dirt road at the hub of a ring of villages halfway between Bunia and the Ugandan border. I was directed to a makeshift town hall where a home-grown adjudication body known locally as La Commission Foncière made up of respected local elders was holding what might be called a judicial hearing. They had been trained, and until the previous year had been paid modest honoraria by the United Nations to travel from town to town and village to village to lay the groundwork for reconciliations to the resentments and claims left behind by the conflict. They adjudicated disputes over land, but since all family and ethnic disputes are in some way related to lands, the three travelling elders and adjudicators were general peacemakers. Lubanga's brutal legacy lurked behind every case. It was raining that day in the town of Fataki, making the yellow mud slippery and the roads impassable. There was no question we would be forced to find a room overnight on the grounds of the nearby church. The rain made no difference to the hearing, the town hall was full. The three judges were adjudicating an important case involving a plot of land the Lendu had seized from a Hema group in retaliation against Lubanga's aggressions that had forced the Hema group to relocate twenty kilometres away.

Both sides were there – those who had seized lands in the heat of the conflict and those who had lost lands and had to move their homes some hills away. Seven years ago, instead of this palaver, there would have been the crackling of gunfire, the thud of machetes, blood, and young boys with dead eyes. Instead I found three jurists, one from the Lendu, one from the Hema, and a third from the Aru, three temperate, thoughtful, well-spoken gentlemen of the region. They blamed no one in the case. It was difficult for the parties to keep calm when talking about their lost lands and lives, but they did, keeping faith that an accord would come one day, if only they were patient. The modest stipends for these paralegals had come to an end a few months before, and still they made the circuit from threats to disputes to palavers and eventually adjudication as a service to the people. They did so with little bravado and, as far as I could tell, hardly any recompense.

Raindrops drilled small brown craters on the ground as we adjourned after a two-hour session and went our separate ways. The UN vehicle was waiting to carry us to the church. The three jurists protested when we offered a lift: they said the vehicle would likely get stuck en route where they were going and, in any event, they expected to make a stop in town at the house of a family with a case to review. I was struck by the lack of pretence and posturing among these Iturians who had little to gain from calling attention to themselves. The discussion in Fataki weighed the claims of victims, though not so much to determine who was and who was not telling the truth, since for the most part everyone knew what had happened. They were all eyewitnesses, and there was no sense making an issue over that. Quarrelling too much with tempers flaring over what had happened would make it more difficult to resolve the issues, and besides, the idea was to quell rather than ignite tempers.

Before leaving Bunia, I visited another outpost of peace-building, the local offices of the International Criminal Court perched high above the town on a hill that had previously been an armed forces base. It was out of the way and well-protected for obvious reasons; as far as many people in town were concerned, the ICC was putting a local hero on trial for defending their homeland, and that made the place a target for Lubanga's leftover Hema militia. I doubt many people would have wanted to be seen frequenting the Court's fortress on the hill. The offices were well-appointed strategically behind a strong enclosure and blocks of offices and lodgings for esteemed visitors from the Court. There was a small communications centre on site where the kindly

Nicholas Kiyaku was in charge and went on public radio every week to explain the progress of the trial, though he doubted many people were listening.

The comparison was inescapable: Fataki and The Hague's outpost on the hill, the town hall meeting and Chamber One at the ICC. They were both worthy, and I do not claim that the three country jurists could do in any measure what the Court with its lofty buildings could. They are different on most counts. And yet there were lessons from the three humble jurists. Humility was the first one obviously, a scarce quality in The Hague. Those who had been victimized or suffered losses in the conflict were primary participants in the town hall, and this was another striking difference; the victims in the Lubanga trial held only the most peripheral position, and when they tried to lodge common sense appeals to expand the charges against Lubanga, the mandarins of the Court gave them little credence. Here, the injured parties held centre stage. And the process was conciliatory. There had been enough fighting and there were better ways to resolve their differences.

After Lubanga's sentencing on 10 July 2012, legal manoeuvring continued as the two sides prepared for the inevitable appeal. The defence argued that Thomas Lubanga had been wrongly convicted and should serve no sentence at all, while the prosecution argued the sentence was "manifestly inadequate and disproportionate to the gravity of the crime."[2] They filed their respective submissions on 3 December 2012, hardly six months following the conclusion of the trial. The defence reiterated its claim that none of the nine soldier witnesses were credible, that none could be shown to be under fifteen, and therefore none were really child soldiers. The prosecution argued the sentence did not take into account the extent of Lubanga's responsibility or the full scope of his crimes. The Appeals Chamber deliberated for two years and concluded on 1 December 2014 there was no need for a change in the verdict or the sentencing.

There happened to be two other trials underway at the same time involving defendants who had fought against Lubanga in the Ituri wars, Ngudjolo Chui and Germain "Simba" Katanga. Although the crimes and circumstances of all three were relatively similar, their fates were strikingly different. Ngudjolo Chui was acquitted for reasons that remain cloudy. Germain Katanga was convicted on a number of counts and sentenced to twelve years in prison. Unlike Lubanga, however, Germain Katanga had readily and often expressed regret for his crimes and apologized to the victims. Shortly after his sentencing, Germain Katanga asked the Court to approve his release or, at the minimum, reduce his sentence, and on 13 November 2015, three judges did in fact decide to reduce his sentence by three years and eight months.

Thomas Lubanga followed suit. He appealed to the Court for release or to have his sentence similarly reduced. His defence counsellor argued for a release on the basis of good behaviour. Lubanga himself promised, in his brief to the judges, that he would enrol in a PhD program at the University of Kisangani and would study the psycho-sociological determinants of conflicts in the DRC with the intent to use what he learned to promote reconciliation in Ituri. The judges did not believe him; on 22 September 2015 the three judges decided that his appeal was unjustified. Although Judge Fulford had been inclined towards leniency in Lubanga's case, other judges who subsequently reconsidered the trial and evidence were not so inclined. Prison time was not reduced. He would have to wait two years before trying again.

There was then an unusual development. On 19 December 2015, the ICC announced it had agreed to a request by both Germain Katanga and Thomas Lubanga to allow them to serve the rest of their sentences in the Democratic Republic of Congo. This was surprising, since the military prisons in the DRC are far less comfortable than the prison at Scheveningen, or anywhere else in Europe for that matter, where they might be sent to serve. It was even more unusual because of the possibility that both of them might be tried in a Congolese court for additional charges once they were released from the ICC sentence.

The Court nevertheless agreed. Thomas Lubanga is now serving out his sentence in his home country in a military prison somewhere in the Democratic Republic of Congo.

chapter 17

Afterword

A swarm of questions hovered over the Court in the wake of the trial. There was the question of victim participation: why were they shunted off into a corner? And sexual violence: why was it embargoed? There were questions about why the trial took so long, about how much witness protection is too much and under what circumstances the prosecution can avoid disclosure. But the question that seems at the root of many others is whether the ICC's courtroom procedure with its triumvirate of actors – two adversarial counsellors and a judge presumed to serve as arbiter – is appropriate for getting to the bottom of a conflict episode like the Ituri wars. Heated issues are bound to arise in cases involving social conflict episodes. There are bound to be unique challenges getting to the bottom of the melee of aggressions when the accepted modus operandi in the Chamber is for each of the two sides to support its own view by discrediting the other's. If there are already heated social or political issues in play, putting two sparring counsellors in the ring to sort things out is not likely to do much to wring the truth out of the evidence.

The drafters of the Rome Statute were wise enough to anticipate this. The Rome Statute urged actors in the trial to be more cooperative than combative, and to this end the prosecutor was asked to assume a neutral posture by investigating incriminating and exonerating circumstances of the case in equal measure.

The advice to the prosecution to investigate "incriminating and exonerating circumstances equally" departs richly from common courtroom culture, since it asks the prosecutor to establish both the guilt and the innocence of a defendant. That makes the prosecutor a neutral actor in the trial akin to a *juge d'instruction* in the civil law tradition.[1] The intention is to keep the Chamber from straying into a contest about evidence, as it can in the common law tradition, because when this happens in the course of adjudicating a conflict episode, the truth gets lost in a barrage of courtroom histrionics. The article goes on to ask the prosecutor to be particularly careful in the investigations, "to respect the personal circumstances of the victims and witnesses," because there are bound to be hard feelings. Trials that come before this Court are incendiary affairs and the sensitivities call for a conciliatory process.

The principle of this provision is that the prosecution and defence are to share a common interest, the cause of justice in the wake of a war. One of the ironies of the Lubanga trial is that by ignoring this provision, the actors in the trial showed how correct the drafters were. The oppositional disposition in the Lubanga Chamber did very much what the drafters were afraid of. It drowned out the truth with the noise of confrontation. This perpetual wrangling hung over the Chamber like a malediction that almost no one wanted to acknowledge, since it seemed unworthy of the Court's higher purpose. I recall looking on as if I were a young child witnessing adults fighting with each other and fighting for no reason. If there were a reason, it had become irrelevant. Or because the quarrelling served an unsavoury purpose, and the purpose in this case was not, as common law courts assume, to filter out truths from deceptions. The quarrelling did nothing to get to the heart of the issue. For the defence, it was to discredit the prosecution and to have an edge in the trial, to hold onto a higher ground and seize advantage in the Chamber wars, all of which, as far as I could see, had little to do with having a better understanding of what had happened in Ituri.

My account has had a cynical air, not surprising since it takes place under the storm clouds of the Lubanga trial; but it is not meant to be a denunciation. On the contrary. The beauty of the International Criminal Court is that it was born from a wellspring of conviction that the world needed an instrument to protect citizens from abusive rulers. This narrative about the trial may be critical, but it is written in the spirit of this conviction that, in spite of all its liabilities, the advantages are incalculable. There are threats to the Court functioning in the way it was intended. They crippled the Lubanga trial, and this unsparing account calls attention to these threats. This final chapter focuses on a few critical matters exposed in this troubled first trial and remarks how the Court has responded.

The status of the victims was an issue of special importance. During the trial, the Chamber preferred to keep them on the margins, since none of the actors in the trial wanted to compromise their own personal interests by admitting yet another voice that might bring an unpredictable element into the proceedings. But once the trial was over and after everyone had left, the victims were still there in the corridors waiting to hear about reparations. This was hardly what the Rome Statute had intended. When the verdict announced Lubanga had done nothing wrong to anyone but child soldiers, this meant that only a fraction of those who had gone through the laborious process to qualify as victims could be considered for reparations. Even those who had been child soldiers for whom the verdict paved the way for compensation would have to prove it. The Chamber's main actors had been too busy tussling among themselves to care much about reconciling the social vestiges of the conflict in Ituri by appeasing the victims, even though reparations for the victims should have been, by definition, a central part of the trial. No one seemed to consider seriously that once the proceedings came to an end, the Chamber or someone would then have to see to the broader features of the case, to the grievances left behind by the crimes.

As the case continued beyond the trial proper, amends would have to be made to address the grievances and diminish the tensions that had provoked the multiple harms in the first place. And it was the Chamber that should have set the stage for assessing the human damage, at least for deciding what kind of recompense might be expected for those scores of registered victims.[2] These victims were not gold-diggers. Standing up to Lubanga and the Hema mafia was too risky if all they wanted was a payout.

They were women who had been raped and young men traumatized and debilitated from the experience of fighting as young children. There were young women to treat, young men to counsel,
land disputes to settle – and all this took the Court beyond a simple
judicial mandate into a social appeasement exercise.

Once the trial was over, the judge drafted his *Decision Establishing
the Principles and Procedures To Be Applied to Reparations*,[3] a tedious
tome with his recommendations on how to compensate the victims.
It was thorough enough – Judge Fulford was nothing if not thorough – but it was obvious the question of reparations, like the presence of victims in his courtroom, was more of an afterthought than
a matter of real concern. The judge's approach was to dispense
with the question of reparations as expeditiously as possible.

The victims had every reason to object. They objected first that
the question of reparations had not really been a high priority for
the Trial Chamber. The judge had argued it should not be up to the
Chamber to determine who might qualify for reparations or how
many victims this might involve or what all this was likely to cost;
it was better to farm this job out to a peripheral organ of the Court,
the Trust Fund for Victims. The victims argued it made little sense
for the judge to distance himself from the consequences of his own
verdict and all that had led up to Lubanga's conviction. But that
was the least of their concerns.

It was a far more serious matter for the victims that the judge
had decided to exempt Thomas Lubanga from any financial responsibility for helping the victims. Here was another indication
of the judge's mysterious personal sympathy for the accused. The
judge was now arguing that the man was indigent, with no assets
or property to use for helping the victims, which in his view ab-
solved Lubanga from any financial responsibility. The victims argued that it mattered little whether Thomas Lubanga *could* pay,
since what mattered is that he *should* pay.

The judge may have suspected the victims would object, and as
a consolation he proposed, in lieu of a financial contribution, that
Mr Lubanga might be inclined to make a non-monetary contribution, a symbolic gesture, as it were. Mr Lubanga might consider a
public apology. What about, he mused in his decision, issuing

certificates to the victims that recognized the harm they had experienced? Here the judge was grasping sadly at straws.

There were still other concerns about the judge's decision. He had decided it was preferable to compensate communities rather than to make reparations directly to individuals. The reasoning was hard to decipher, particularly since it was difficult to imagine what the judge meant by communities, since the ex–child soldiers were first and foremost individuals. There was no community there. Most of the child soldiers were now grown and making their way in the streets or coping with the trauma. They had few affiliations, least of all with each other. They were not part of any collectivity to speak of, scattered as they were throughout the region, recovering or not recovering as the case might be, and it made very little sense to speak about reparations for communities or groupings.

The victims' multiple objections challenging the judge's decisions ended up before the Appeals Chamber in the fall of 2012. After a ponderous two and a half years, the Appeals Chamber decided to reject the judge's draft and uphold the side of the victims. The Appeals Chamber agreed that the judge had "erred" in law and judgment on the matter of Lubanga's financial obligation, since no matter how indigent Lubanga might be, he was still as financially responsible as he was criminally responsible. And yes, it was the Trial Chamber that should have assumed responsibility for laying the groundwork for reparations. And no, it was wrong to place the emphasis on communities. Individuals did count and they had to be considered for individual compensation.[4]

But there was one thing the Appeals Chamber would not and could not fix, and that was the dubious verdict, with all the consequences it had for who should be eligible for reparations. The curiously narrow verdict handicapped the reparations process since it said nothing about sexual abuse or the despoiling of lives and property. As far as the verdict was concerned, it was of no consequence how many women had been victimized or how many families had lost property, because the Chamber saw no reason to attribute these things to Lubanga. The only thing he had done wrong was to use child soldiers. It followed that to qualify for reparations, a victim would have to prove he or she had been underage in Lubanga's army at the time, and that would not be easy. The myriad individuals injured in the war had no real right to anything from Lubanga or the international community, not even modest compensation, and this included many of the 139 individuals who had applied to be part of the trial and participated through their legal representatives.

After much debate, it was decided that the Court needed to do something for these victims, even if the trial Chamber's verdict excluded most of them. Even the Appeals Chamber suggested the Court had the option to make its own amends under a separate assistance program for victims, if need be. The Trust Fund for Victims was requested to make up a plan, and in spite of the fact that the formal legal process of the Court had cut off most of the victims from whatever compensation might have been their due, the Trust Fund for Victims had a quasi-autonomous status, and if the relevant articles in the statute were construed appropriately, the fund might consider giving some relief to a broader group of victims than the original verdict allowed.

Bringing victims into the trials of the International Criminal Court was always an ideal. The drafters knew it would mean a change in how the trials in the Court were managed, and they were right, it would be difficult. They were also right that it was the proper thing to do.[5] As of this writing, the matter is still before the Trust Fund for Victims, where it is likely this peripheral organ of the Court will make up for the neglect of the Chamber and offer some compensation, even if it is modest and amounts to only a token assurance that the Court stands for repairing the social fabric in Ituri.

The issue of reparations remains a live and difficult one. Many years may pass before the Court decides to compensate Lubanga's victims, and by then it will be too little in some cases, too late in others. But reparation for victims is not the issue that most discredited the Lubanga trial. The issue that brought down the most criticism upon the Court was its neglect of sexual violence. It loomed so large in the trial by its absence that it became the trial's trademark shame, a conspicuous token of the Chamber's failure to place the substance of Ituri's tragedy above its perpetual legal jousting.

Associate Judge Elizabeth Odio Benito's opinion paper,[6] which showed how sexual violence ought to have figured in the assessment of Lubanga's guilt, was captivating and clear. But it came before the Chamber only at the very end of the trial as a brief dissent from the judge's verdict, too late in the trial to make much of a difference. By that time, it was only a footnote to the trial and not an altogether welcome one. Had she put her views forward earlier, it might have given sexual violence a place in the room. It might even have changed the disposition of the Chamber and allowed the topic to be treated with less disdain.

The Chamber's obstinate neglect of sexual violence did, in the end, have a constructive consequence. The criticism that the Court suffered because of it made it more difficult for future trials to set the matter aside as the Lubanga Chamber had done. Warrant by warrant and trial by trial, sexual violence figured more, as if to make up for its neglect in the first trial.[7] The Court knew better than to let the matter slide. The verdict was done, but there were other trials where the lessons applied.

There were two in particular, those of Matthieu Ngudjolo and Germain Katanga, both rebel leaders from the Ituri wars, and in both cases the charges arose out of similar circumstances. Charges were originally limited to the standard war crimes for both of them, murder and destruction of property, with no mention of sexual violence. As the trials progressed while the Lubanga case was concluding, the charges were broadened in both cases to include sexual slavery as a war crime, and rape as both a war crime and a crime against humanity. Ultimately, the judges decided in the Ngudjolo case to acquit the defendant and in the other, not to base the conviction on charges of sexual violence. But there was no embargo on the topic itself in the Chamber.

Then there was the trial of Jean-Pierre Bemba, another Congolese. He is an imposing boulder of a man, once vice-president of the DR Congo under Kabila, with considerable wealth and a taste for power. He had used his own militia of 1,500 men in 2002 to thwart a coup against his friend and ally Ange-Félix Patassé, president of the neighbouring Central African Republic. His men had gone on a binge of raping and killing innocent victims; he knew about it and still did nothing to stop them. The Office of the Prosecution charged him with committing crimes against humanity and war crimes. Rape was among the charges, and it was the first time in history a criminal court adjudicated a rape case under international law. He was found guilty of all charges in June 2016.

Finally, there is the ongoing trial of the infamous Bosco Ntaganda. Ntaganda had been Lubanga's deputy in the Ituri wars, and arrest warrants had been issued for the two of them together in 2006, charging both with the one crime of recruiting child soldiers. Years passed. Lubanga was arrested and taken to The Hague. Bosco Ntaganda meanwhile spent five years flaunting his freedom, pillaging at will with rebel groups of his own making, playing golf in Goma, and doing as he pleased under Rwandan military protection. When Rwanda withdrew support and Ntaganda had little choice but to give himself up, he was arrested and brought to The Hague. By the time his charges were confirmed in February 2014, a more mature Court had altered his warrant to include crimes against humanity, including rape and multiple war crimes, with specific reference to sexual slavery and rape. The Court would no longer turn a blind eye to sexual violence.

In good time and perhaps before anyone might have anticipated, the Court has reconsidered these stands taken in the Lubanga case, the issue of reparations and sexual violence most notably, and amends have been made. Trial Chambers now recognize that limiting the participation of victims will, in the end, limit the ability of the Court to achieve restorative justice, and this, after all, is at the core of the Court's mission. A Chamber will also think twice before sacrificing the charge of sexual abuse on the altar of convenience. Progress has been made.

Finally there is the inflammatory matter of investigations, of what is expected and what is proscribed in the way the Court gathers information, and especially how to use intermediaries. It had been a divisive and delicate issue in the Lubanga Chamber.[8] It is a thornier issue than the others, partially because it is less tangible; there is no obvious way of making sure that all evidence comes to the Court untainted. It may also be that the controversy about the role of intermediaries that swirled throughout the Lubanga trial made it more of a problem than it really was. The Court, to its credit, responded as best it could.

Investigations really ought to be straightforward. It is a matter of gathering responses to some basic questions, and as long as there are documents or persons who might have some of these answers, it is a matter of finding them. In the Lubanga courtroom, the matter ended up being convoluted. Maître Mabille used the ways the prosecution had assembled evidence as a truncheon in the Chamber to batter the prosecution and their witnesses. She proclaimed the prosecution was hiding evidence that could have been used to prove Lubanga's innocence. She proclaimed the prosecution's investigators in Ituri never really took the gathering of information seriously. She claimed that instead of collecting evidence themselves, the investigators hired local agents to collect information for them and were complacent in managing them. These were the intermediaries who, she claimed, distorted evidence by telling witnesses what to say when they came to Court. It all amounted to a claim by Maître Mabille and her team that the prosecution was conspiring to distort evidence in a plot to deceive the Chamber.

It is very difficult for anyone to say just how neglectful the prosecution had been or, as Maître Mabille would repeatedly contend, whether the Office of the Prosecution had ever conspired to deliberately distort the evidence. Both the defence and the judge wanted the Chamber to believe that the prosecution, their investigators, and local agents were liars and should be roundly punished. It was a mess, and the mess so permeated the trial that it rendered any objective understanding of the facts nearly impossible. The probable truth is that the assertions were inflated, which is not to say the testimony of the witnesses brought in by the intermediaries was free of inconsistences; there were inconsistencies, and maybe even full-fledged lies, but they were not part of a systematic scheme to deceive the Chamber.

The judge nevertheless became convinced the prosecution had deliberately dispensed with legal propriety and had neglected its responsibility as an investigator.[9] He was uncommonly vocal about it. The intense debate about the prosecution's failure to get proper evidence has led legal professionals, inside and outside the Court, to reflect on sharing evidence in international criminal trials and especially on the use of intermediaries in conducting investigations. The Office of the Prosecution had already received its share of rebukes, starting with the judge's unrelenting disapproval, and this has set the tone for subsequent commentary. Legal academics have argued that the prosecution botched the investigation and never had any idea what it was getting into with the intermediaries, that the investigators were afraid to go into the communities themselves and they cared more about their own safety than about getting reliable testimony.[10]

In 2011, with the Lubanga trial still underway, the Court struck a working group to reflect on the state of intermediary affairs and issued a *Draft Guidelines on the Relationship between the Court and the Intermediaries*[11] to set standards for the Court's use of local agents. The guidelines came out as a formal Court document somewhat later, in March 2014. If nothing else, the document is indicative of a Court that wants to ward off its missteps by making clear what the right steps are in the first place. It would be nice if the case of intermediaries were that simple. The difficulties the Court's organs have faced and will continue to face in gathering information will be as various as the local agents they select, the functions they are expected to perform, and the different political atmospheres region to region, maybe even community to community. The guidelines confess as much in the introduction, allowing that "variations in the use of and approach to intermediaries mean that Court-wide standardization of all aspects concerning intermediaries may not be possible."[12] It was to the Court's credit that it began with this caveat, especially because standardization may not really be feasible.

The Court has done what it can to address the strident protests about investigations that occurred in the Lubanga trial, and at least the guidelines stand for the Court's concern about using local agents to learn about war zones. What the Court has now learned is that gathering information cannot be taken for granted. Investigators have to be monitored and supported, and their relations with sources of evidence have to be open for inspection. At the same time, the Court must accept that the guidelines will probably do little to purge the process of all contentious issues. It would have done little to satisfy Maître Mabille's complaint that the prosecutor's use of intermediaries sullied the trial irremediably. The intermediaries did some unexpected things, and some were regrettable, but they were not responsible for the wholesale failure of the evidence in the Lubanga Chamber. That was as much, if not more attributable to the actors in the courtroom, Maître Mabille especially, who used the role of local agents as a weapon in the Chamber wars. Maître Mabille's reckless assertions, undeterred by the judge, did more to misrepresent information on Lubanga's guilt than one or two errant intermediaries did.

~

The Lubanga Chamber seemed to lose touch with those it was to serve. Victims were relegated to the margins. The worst atrocities were excluded for procedural reasons, while the minutiae of the law and the professional practice and ambitions of celebrated criminal lawyers led the trial into a chrysalis of its own where the main actors, in pursuing their own interests, became less and less accountable to the ideals of global justice. There were instances in which the Chamber, instead of protecting vulnerable citizens, was more concerned to protect the law itself and its practitioners. This book has shown the fault lines in the Chamber that allowed the Court's humanitarian mission to fade into the background while other less important matters came to the fore. The trial did not end well. Lubanga was never asked to fully account for the worst of his crimes, and the harms inflicted on his victims have been, until now, set aside.

Meanwhile, the story of the International Criminal Court continues and with distinctly more positive prospects. There was no obligation for the Court to address the welter of concerns that came out of the Lubanga trial, but it did. It could have retreated into a legal cocoon. But there is something everyone learns while becoming more familiar with the Court, and it is that this otherwise austere legal edifice with its well-appointed Chambers has a large and loyal global fan base. This is curious at first; there are not many international bodies with such a robust following, and this following is not just the standard prominent sponsors. There are hundreds of volunteer organizations, citizen groups, celebrities, NGOs who have been partners and collaborators from the ICC's inception, private sector backers, a majority of states, and an abundance of small and large international bodies who want the Court to work. There are also countless concerned individuals. A Kenyan acquaintance of mine who manages a shop on the outskirts of Nairobi speaks passionately about how he wants the Court to work. The third-generation Greek owners of Le Hellenique in Ituri's capital Bunia raised a glass to salute the work of the Court at our table. A pair of teachers in a school for refugees near Dohuk in northern Kurdistan are counting on the Court to reduce the suffering of displaced persons. I myself want the Court to work. We are not a special or contrived group in any way, just a collection of individuals on different continents who are convinced the Court is what the world needs.

The Court is mindful of this following, and when the Lubanga trial took decisions that seemed to betray the values they expect the Court to uphold, they said so. Judges may not be comfortable with the presence of Court supporters in the wings, especially when their positions interfere with those procedures on which judges rely to protect their authority in the Chamber, though there is no disputing they have been invaluable assets. They supported the prosecutor when the Chamber appeared to veer dangerously towards acquitting Lubanga by making their presence known during the closing arguments. They have supported the Court's decisions on being more attentive to sexual violence and the role of victims. They have warned investigators to be more thorough in gathering evidence. They are a healthy antidote when a Chamber shows signs of closing itself off from the public, as the Lubanga Chamber did when the judge stringently warned the prosecution against discussing the trial with the press, what he derisively referred to as "satellite litigation."

The story now continues, as there are new cases and new trials and potentially ones more complex than the Lubanga one. Heads of state may soon appear at the Court instead of regional warlords like Lubanga, and when this happens, the stakes in the trials will be even higher than they were in the Lubanga courtroom. The Court's mandate to serve its constituencies of global citizens will become even more demanding and urgent than it is now, and when this happens it will need even more those it serves to be as passionately a part of the Court as they have been in the past.

Notes

Introduction

1 Gerard Prunier, "The Ethnic Confict in Ituri District," in *The Recurring Great Lakes Crisis: Identity, Violence and Power*, ed. Jean-Pierre Chretien and Richard Banegas (London: Hurst Publishers, 2009), 195.

Chapter 2

1 Gérard Prunier, *Africa's World War: Congo, the Rwandan Genocide, and the Making of a Continental Catastrophe* (Oxford: Oxford University Press, 2009). Prunier's is arguably the best book on the war, though Stearns's *Dancing in the Glory of Monsters* is a smart and colourful read: see Jason K. Stearns, *Dancing in the Glory of Monsters: The Collapse of the Congo and the Great War of Africa* (New York: PublicAffairs, 2011).

2 Dan Fahey, *Ituri: Gold, Land and Ethnicity in Northeastern Congo* (Nairobi: Rift Valley Institute, Usalama Project, 2013), summarizes the background to the conflict. It may be supplemented by Chris Huggins, *Land, Power and Identity: Roots of Violent Conflict in Eastern DRCC* (Brussels: International Alert, November 2010).

3 The Panel of Experts report on the Congo for 2002 describes how Uganda's alliances for economic gain wreaked social havoc in Ituri: United Nations Security Council, *Final Report of the Panel of Experts on the Illegal Exploitation of Natural Resources and Other Forms of Wealth of the Democratic Republic of the Congo*, S2002/1146, 16 October 2002.

Chapter 3

1 Human Rights Watch, *Ituri: "Covered in Blood," Ethnically Targeted Violence in Northeastern DR Congo: Massacres and Other Human Rights Abuses* 15, no. 11(A), 8 July 2003, 23.

Chapter 4

1 For an unembellished account of this turn of events, see United Nations Security Council, *Special Report on the Events in Ituri, January 2002– December 2003*, Security Council S/2004/573, 16 July 2004.

2 Two of the most straightforward accounts for the events described here and in subsequent paragraphs are Gerard Prunier, "The 'Ethnic' Conflict in Ituri District," in *The Recurring Great Lakes Crisis: Identity, Violence and Power*, ed. Jean-Pierre Chretien and Richard Banegas, 180–204 (London: Hurst Publishers, 1968); Human Rights Watch, *Ituri: "Covered in Blood," Ethnically Targeted Violence in Northeastern DR Congo* 15, no. 11(A), July 2003.

3 Human Rights Watch, *Ituri: "Covered in Blood,"* 29.

4 Kees Homan, "Operation Artemis in the Democratic Republic of the Congo," in *European Commission: Faster and More United? The Debate about Europe's Crisis Response Capacity*, ed. Andrea Ricci and Eero Kytömaa, 151–5 (Bloomington: Indiana University Press, 2006).

5 Henning Tamm, *UPC in Ituri: The External Militarization of Local Politics in North-eastern Congo* (Nairobi: Rift Valley Institute, 2013), 42.

6 There are many accounts of the evolution and creation of the court. Among the more useful are William A. Schabas, *An Introduction to the International Criminal Court*, 2nd ed. (Cambridge: Cambridge University Press, 2001); Benjamin N. Schiff, *Building the International Criminal Court* (Cambridge: Cambridge University Press, 2008).

7 Kofi Annan, *We the Peoples: The Role of the United Nations in the 21st Century* (New York: United Nations, Department of Public Information, 2000), 48.

Chapter 5

1 Thomas Lubanga could have reasonably been charged with those offences currently confirmed for his co-perpetrator, Bosco Ntaganda: thirteen counts of war crimes (murder and attempted murder, attacking civilians, rape, sexual slavery of civilians, pillaging, displacement of civilians, attacking protected objects, destroying enemy property, and rape, sexual slavery, enlistment, and conscription of child soldiers under age fifteen) and five counts of crimes against humanity (murder and attempted murder, rape, sexual slavery, persecution, forcible transfer of population).

2 Valerie Oosterveld, "The Special Court for Sierra Leone, Child Soldiers, and Forced Marriage: Providing Clarity or Confusion?" *Canadian Yearbook of International Law*, 2007, 131–72.

3 Susan McKay and Dyan Mazurana, *Where Are the Girls? Girls in Fighting Forces in Northern Uganda, Sierra Leone and Mozambique: Their Lives during*

and after War (Saint-Lazare, QC: International Centre for Human Rights and Democratic Development [Rights and Democracy], 2004).

4 Tonderai W. Chikuhwa, "The Evolution of the United Nations Protection Agenda for Children: Applying International Standards," in *Child Soldiers in the Age of Fractured States*, ed. Scott Gates and Simon Reich, 37–51 (Pittsburgh: University of Pittsburgh Press, 2010); Matthew Hoppold, "Child Recruitment as a Crime under the Rome Statute of the International Criminal Court," in *The International Regime of the International Criminal Court: Essays in Honour of Igor Blischenko*, ed. Jose Doria, Hans-Peter Gasser, and M. Cherif Bassiouini, 579–608, International Humanitarian Law Series (Leiden: Martinus Nijhoff Publishers, 2009).

5 Article 77 (2) Additional Protocol I, Geneva Convention; and Article 38, Convention on the Rights of the Child, 1990.

6 Graca Machel, *The Impact of War on Children* (London: C. Hurst, 2001).

7 Human Rights Watch, "DR Congo: ICC Charges Raise Concerns – Joint Letter to the Chief Prosecutor of the International Criminal Court," 31 July 2006, https://www.hrw.org/news/2006/07/31/dr-congo-icc -charges-raise-concernsQ1.

Chapter 6

1 Schabas, *An Introduction to the International Criminal Court*, 126; Morten Bergsmo and Pieter Kruger, "Article 54," in *Commentary on the Rome Statute of the International Criminal Court: Observers' Notes, Article by Article*, ed. Otto Triffterer (Baden-Baden: Nomos Verlagsgesellschaft, 1999), 716.

2 Article 54, 3(e).

3 For a comprehensive review of the witness protection regime at the ICC, see Human Rights Watch, *Courting History: The Landmark International Criminal Court's First Years* (New York: Human Rights Watch, 2008).

Chapter 9

1 *Prosecutor*, documentary, dir. Barry Stevens, 1 hr 34 min, White Pine Pictures, 2010. http://www.whitepinepictures.com/all-titles/ijd-the -prosecutor/.

Chapter 10

1 Operation Artemis.

Chapter 11

1 For useful summaries of the history, rationale, and practice of bringing victims before the International Criminal Court, see Christine Van den Wyngaert, "Victims before International Criminal Courts: Some Views and Concerns of ICC Trial Judge," *Case Western Reserve Journal of International Law* 44, no. 1 (2011): 475–96; Luke Moffett, *Realizing Justice for Victims before the International Criminal Court*, International Crimes Database (ICD), ICD Series #6, 2014.
2 Regulation 55.
3 Anja Wiersing, "Lubanga and Its Implications for Victims Seeking Reparations at the International Criminal Court," *Amsterdam Law Forum* 4, no. 3 (2012): 21–39.

Chapter 13

1 International Justice Monitor, "Interview: ICC Prosecutors Will Refute Allegations That Intermediaries Manipulated Evidence in Lubanga Case," 15 March 2010, https://www.ijmonitor.org/2010/03/interview -icc-prosecutors-will-refute-allegations-that-intermediaries-manipulated -evidence-in-lubanga-case/.
2 Prosecutor v Thomas Lubanga Dyilo, Public Document: ICC-01/04-01/06, *Decision on the Press Interview with Ms Le Fraper du Hellen*, 12 May 2010.
3 The compatibility of peace and justice is less obvious than it would seem on first glance, as evidenced in Janine Natalya Clark, "Peace, Justice, and the International Criminal Court: Limitations and Possibilities," *Journal of International Criminal Justice* 9 (2011): 521–45; see also Linda M. Keller, "The False Dichotomy of Peace versus Justice at the International Criminal Court," *Hague Justice Journal* 3, no. 1 (2008): 12–47.
4 Tim Allen, *Trial Justice: The International Criminal Court and the Lord's Resistance Army* (London: Zed Books, in association with International African Institute, 2006).

Chapter 14

1 Christian de Vos, "Prosecutor v Lubanga: 'Someone Who Comes between One Person and Another': Lubanga, Local Cooperation and the Right to a Fair Trial," *Melbourne Journal of International Law* 12, no. 1 (2011): 217.
2 William Schabas, quoted in Marlise Simon, "For International Criminal Court, Frustration and Missteps in Its First Trial," *New York Times*, 22 November 2010.
3 Suspicions about the role of intermediaries in the Lubanga trial has turned the rather practical matter of using local informants to gather evidence

into a hotly debated theoretical issue on the pros and cons of outsourcing investigations. The following are sample articles from a long list: Elena Baylis, "Outsourcing Investigations," *UCLA Journal of International Law and Foreign Affairs* 121 (2009): 121–47; Open Society Justice Initiative, *Intermediaries and the International Criminal Court: A Role for the Assembly of States Parties* (New York: December 2011); and Danya Chakiel, "The Prosecutor v Thomas Lubanga Dyilo: A Turbulent but Promising Retrospective," The Hague Justice Portal, 17 November 2011, http://www.haguejusticeportal.net/index.php?id=12987.

4 Gil Courtemanche, *Le Monde, Le lézard et moi* (Montreal: Éditions de Boréal, 2009).

5 Prosecutor v Thomas Lubanga Dyilo, Appeals Chamber Ruling: ICC-01/04-01/06 OA17, 8 October 2010.

Chapter 15

1 Human Rights Watch, *Ending Impunity for Sexual Violence in the Democratic Republic of Congo: New Judicial Mechanism Needed to Bring Perpetrators to Justice*, 10 June 2014; see also United Nations Human Rights Office of the High Commissioner and MONUSCO, "DRC: Some Progress in the Fight against Impunity but Rape Still Widespread and Largely Unpunished – UN Report," 9 April 2014, http://www.ohchr.org/EN/NewsEvents/Pages/DisplayNews.aspx?NewsID=14489&#sthash.yMA3W8ri.dpuf.

2 Human Rights Watch, *Seeking Justice: The Prosecution of Sexual Violence in the Congo War* 17, no. 1(A) (2005), http://www.ohchr.org/EN/NewsEvents/Pages/DisplayNews.aspx?NewsID=14489&#sthash.yMA3W8ri.dpuf.

3 Robert Garreton, *Democratic Republic of Congo: Report of the Mapping Report Exercise Documenting the Most Serious Violations of Human Rights and International Humanitarian Law* (New York: United Nations Human Rights Commission, Office of the High Commissioner, 2010).

4 Elizabeth Odio Benito, *Separate and Dissenting Opinion of Judge Odio Benito*, International Criminal Court, Prosecutor v Thomas Lubanga Dyilo, ICC-01/04-01/06-2842, 14 March 2012, 8.

5 Ibid., 7.

Chapter 16

1 The drafters of the Rome Statute were aware of risks in allowing the common law tradition to exclusively govern the management of international trials. Article 54, 1(a) was proposed in order to insert an element of the Continental law tradition hoping to temper the adversarial encounter

between defence and prosecution by making the prosecution more of a "neutral" actor in the trial. This article was largely ignored in the Lubanga trial. See Caroline Buisman, "The Prosecutor's Obligation to Investigate Incriminating and Exonerating Circumstances Equally: Illusion or Reality?" *Leiden Journal of International Law* 27, no. 1 (2014): 205–26.

2 Prosecution v Thomas Lubanga Dyilo, Appeals Chamber, *Prosecution's Document in Support of Appeal against the "Decision on Sentence pursuant to Article 76 of the Statute,"* ICC-01/04-01/06-2950, 3 December 2012.

Chapter 17

1 Morten Bergsmo and Pieter Kruger, "Article 54," in *Commentary on the Rome Statute of the International Criminal Court: Observers' Notes, Article by Article,* ed. Otto Triffterer, 1077–87 (Baden-Baden: Nomos Verlagsgesellschaft, 1999).

2 Wiersing, "Lubanga and Its Implication for Victims Seeking Reparations."

3 Adrian Fulford, Elizabeth Odio Benito, and René Blattman, *Decision Establishing the Principles and Procedures to Be Applied to Reparations,* Situation in the Democratic Republic of the Congo, the Case of the Prosecutor v Thomas Lubanga Dyilo, International Criminal Court, No. ICC-01/04-01/06, 7 August 2012.

4 The Appeals Chamber, Judgment on the Appeals against the *"Decision Establishing the Principles and Procedures to Be Applied to Reparations" of 7 August 2012 with AMENDED Order for Reparations (Annex A) and Public Annexes 1 and 2,* Situation in the Democratic Republic of the Congo in the Case of the Prosecutor v Thomas Lubanga Dyilo, ICC-01/04-01/06 A A 2 A 3, 3 March 2015.

5 Carsten Stahn, "Reparative Justice after the Lubanga Appeals Judgment on Principles and Procedures of Reparation," EJIL Talk! Blog of the *European Journal of International Law,* 7 April 2015, https://www.ejiltalk.org/reparative-justice-after-the-lubanga-appeals-judgment-on-principles-and-procedures-of-reparation/.

6 Elizabeth Odio Benito, *Separate and Dissenting Opinion of Judge Odio Benito,* International Criminal Court, the Case of Thomas Lubanga Dyilo v The Prosecutor, ICC-01/04-01/06-2842, 14 March 2012, 8–9.

7 Susanne SáCounto and Katherine Cleary, "The Importance of Effective Investigation of Sexual Violence and Gender Based Crimes at the International Criminal Court," *American University Journal of Gender, Social Policy and the Law* 17, no. 337 (2009): 338–58.

8 Caroline Buisman, "Delegating Investigations: Lessons to Be Learned from the Lubanga Judgment," *Northwestern Journal of Human Rights* 11, no. 3 (2013): 29–82.

9 Judges Adrian Fulford, Elizabeth Odio Benito, and René Blattman, *Hearing to Deliver the Decision Pursuant to Article 76 in the Case of the Prosecutor v Thomas Lubanga Dyilo, ICC-01/04-01/06*, International Criminal Court, 10 July 2012, 3–9.

10 Buisman, "Prosecutor's Obligation to Investigate Incriminating and Exonerating Circumstances Equally."

11 International Criminal Court, *Guidelines Governing the Relations between the Court and Intermediaries for the Organs and Units of the Court and Counsel Working with Intermediaries* (The Hague: ICC, 2014).

12 Ibid., 3.

Bibliography

Allen, Tim. *Trial Justice: The International Criminal Court and the Lord's Resistance Army*. London: Zed Books, in association with International African Institute, 2006.

Annan, Kofi. *We the Peoples: The Role of the United Nations in the 21st Century*. New York: United Nations, Department of Public Information, 2000.

Appeals Chamber. Judgment on the Appeals against the *"Decision Establishing the Principles and Procedures to Be Applied to Reparations" of 7 August 2012 with AMENDED Order for Reparations (Annex A) and Public Annexes 1 and 2*. Situation in the Democratic Republic of the Congo in the Case of the Prosecutor v Thomas Lubanga Dyilo, ICC-01/04-01/06 A A 2 A 3, 3 March 2015.

Baylis, Elena. "Outsourcing Investigations." *UCLA Journal of International Law and Foreign Affairs* 121 (2009): 121–47.

Benito, Elizabeth Odio. *Separate and Dissenting Opinion of Judge Odio Benito*. International Criminal Court, the Case of Thomas Lubanga Dyilo v The Prosecutor, ICC-01/04-01/06-2842, 14 March 2012.

Bergsmo, Morten, and Pieter Kruger. "Article 54." In *Commentary on the Rome Statute of the International Criminal Court: Observers' Notes, Article by Article*, ed. Otto Triffterer, 1077–87. Baden-Baden: Nomos Verlagsgesellschaft, 1999.

Buisman, Caroline. "Delegating Investigations: Lessons to Be Learned from the Lubanga Judgment." *Northwestern Journal of Human Rights* 11, no. 3 (2013): 29–82.

– "The Prosecutor's Obligation to Investigate Incriminating and Exonerating Circumstances Equally: Illusion or Reality?" *Leiden Journal of International Law* 27, no. 1 (2014): 205–26.

Chakiel, Danya. "The Prosecutor v Thomas Lubanga Dyilo: A Turbulent but Promising Retrospective." The Hague Justice Portal, 17 November 2011. http://www.haguejusticeportal.net/index.php?id=12987.

Chikuhwa, Tonderai W. "The Evolution of the United Nations Protection Agenda for Children: Applying International Standards." In *Child Soldiers in the Age of Fractured States*, ed. Scott Gates and Simon Reich, 37–51. Pittsburgh: University of Pittsburgh Press, 2010.

Courtemanche, Gil. *Le Monde, le lézard et moi*. Montreal: Editions de Boréal, 2009.

Fahey, Dan. "Guns and Butter: Uganda's Involvement in Northeastern Congo 2003–2009." In *L'Afrique des Grands Lacs*, Annuaire 2009–2010, ed. S. Marysse, F. Reyntjens, and S. Vandeginste, 343–70. Paris: L'Harmattan, 2010.

– *Ituri: Gold, Land and Ethnicity in Northeastern Congo*. Nairobi: Usalama Project, Rift Valley Institute, 2013.

– "The Trouble with Ituri." *African Security Review* 20, no. 2 (2011): 108–13.

Fulford, Adrian, Elizabeth Odio Benito, and René Blattman. *Decision Establishing the Principles and Procedures to Be Applied to Reparations*. Situation in the Democratic Republic of the Congo, the Case of the Prosecutor v Thomas Lubanga Dyilo. International Criminal Court, No. ICC-01/04-01/06, 7 August 2012.

– *Hearing to Deliver the Decision Pursuant to Article 76 in the Case of the Prosecutor v Thomas Lubanga Dyilo, ICC-01/04-01/06*. International Criminal Court, 10 July 2012, 3–9.

Grotius, Hugo. *The Law of War and Peace*, trans. Francis Kelsey. Oxford: Oxford University Press, 1925. Originally published in 1625.

Homan, Kees. "Operation Artemis in the Democratic Republic of the Congo." In *European Commission: Faster and More United? The Debate about Europe's Crisis Response Capacity*, ed. Andrea Ricci and Eero Kytömaa, 151–5. Bloomington: Indiana University Press, 2006.

Hoppold, Matthew. "Child Recruitment as a Crime under the Rome Statute of the International Criminal Court." In *The International Regime of the International Criminal Court: Essays in Honour of Igor Blischenko*, ed. Jose Doria, Hans-Peter Gasser, and M. Cherif Bassiouini, 579–608, International Humanitarian Law Series. Leiden: Martinus Nijhoff Publishers, 2009.

Huggins, Chris. *Land, Power and Identity: Roots of Violent Conflict in Eastern DRC*. Brussels: International Alert, November 2010.

Human Rights Watch. *Courting History: The Landmark International Criminal Court's First Years*. New York: Human Rights Watch, 2008.

– "DR Congo: ICC Charges Raise Concerns – Joint Letter to the Chief Prosecutor of the International Criminal Court," 31 July 2006. https://www.hrw.org/news/2006/07/31/dr-congo-icc-charges-raise-concern.

- *Ending Impunity for Sexual Violence in the Democratic Republic of Congo: New Judicial Mechanism Needed to Bring Perpetrators to Justice*, 10 June 2014.
- *Ituri: "Covered in Blood," Ethnically Targeted Violence in Northeastern DR Congo* 15, no. 11(A), 8 July 2003.
- *Seeking Justice: The Prosecution of Sexual Violence in the Congo War* 17, no. 1(A), March 2005.

International Criminal Court. *Guidelines Governing the Relations between the Court and Intermediaries for the Organs and Units of the Court and Counsel Working with Intermediaries*. The Hague: ICC, March 2014.

International Justice Monitor. "Interview: ICC Prosecutors Will Refute Allegations That Intermediaries Manipulated Evidence in Lubanga Case," 15 March 2010. https://www.ijmonitor.org/2010/03/interview-icc -prosecutors-will-refute-allegations-that-intermediaries-manipulated -evidence-in-lubanga-case/.

Keller, Linda M. "The False Dichotomy of Peace versus Justice at the International Criminal Court." *Hague Justice Journal* 3, no. 1 (2008): 12–47.

Machel, Graca. *The Impact of War on Children*. London: C. Hurst, 2001.

McKay, Susan, and Dyan Mazurana. *Where Are the Girls? Girls in Fighting Forces in Northern Uganda, Sierra Leone and Mozambique: Their Lives during and after War*. Saint-Lazare, QC: International Centre for Human Rights and Democratic Development (Rights and Democracy), 2004.

Moffett, Luke. *Realizing Justice for Victims before the International Criminal Court*. International Crimes Database (ICD), ICD series #6, 2014.

Oosterveld, Valerie. "The Special Court for Sierra Leone, Child Soldiers, and Forced Marriage: Providing Clarity or Confusion?" *Canadian Yearbook of International Law*, 2007, 131–72.

Open Society Justice Initiative. *Intermediaries and the International Criminal Court: A Role for the Assembly of States Parties*. New York: OSJI, December 2011.

Prosecutor. Documentary, dir. Barry Stevens, 1 hr 34 min (White Pine Pictures, 2010). http://www.whitepinepictures.com/all-titles/ijd -the-prosecutor/.

Prunier, Gérard. *Africa's World War: Congo, the Rwandan Genocide, and the Making of a Continental Catastrophe*. Oxford: Oxford University Press, 2009.
- "The 'Ethnic' Conflict in Ituri District." In *The Recurring Great Lakes Crisis: Identity, Violence and Power*, ed. Jean-Pierre Chretien and Richard Banegas, 180–204. London: Hurst Publishers, 1968.

SáCounto, Suzanne, and Katherine Cleary. "The Importance of Effective Investigation of Sexual Violence and Gender-Based Crimes at the

International Criminal Court." *American University Journal of Gender, Social Policy and the Law* 17, no. 337 (2009): 338–58.

Schiff, Benjamin N. *Building the International Criminal Court*. Cambridge: Cambridge University Press, 2008.

Simon, Marlise. "For International Criminal Court, Frustration and Missteps in Its First Trial." *New York Times*, 22 November 2010.

Stahn, Carsten. "Reparative Justice after the Lubanga Appeals Judgment on Principles and Procedures of Reparation." EJIL Talk! Blog of the *European Journal of International Law*, 7 April 2015. https://www.ejiltalk.org/ reparative-justice-after-the-lubanga-appeals-judgment-on-principles -and-procedures-of-reparation/.

Stearns, Jason K. *Dancing in the Glory of Monsters: The Collapse of the Congo and the Great War of Africa*. New York: PublicAffairs, 2011.

Tamm, Henning. *UPC in Ituri: The External Militarization of Local Politics in North-eastern Congo*. Nairobi: Rift Valley Institute, 2013.

United Nations Human Rights Office of the High Commissioner and MONUSCO. "DRC: Some Progress in the Fight against Impunity but Rape still Widespread and Largely Unpunished – UN Report," 9 April 2014. http://www.ohchr.org/EN/NewsEvents/Pages/DisplayNews.aspx? NewsID=14489%26#sthash.yMA3W8ri.dpuf.

United Nations Security Council. *Final Report of the Panel of Experts on the Illegal Exploitation of Natural Resources and Other Forms of Wealth of the Democratic Republic of the Congo*. S2002/1146, 16 October 2002.

– *Special Report on the Events in Ituri, January 2002–December 2003*. Security Council S/2004/573, 16 July 2004.

Van den Wyngaert, Christine. "Victims before International Criminal Courts: Some Views and Concerns of ICC Trial Judge." *Case Western Reserve Journal of International Law* 44, no. 1 (2011): 475–96.

Wiersing, Anja. "Lubanga and Its Implication for Victims Seeking Reparations at the International Criminal Court." *Amsterdam Law Forum* 4, no. 3 (2012): 21–39.

Index